India Under the Shadow of Terrorism

India Under the Shadow of Terrorism

H. Parameshwar Hegde

Kaveri Books
New Delhi - 110 002

First Published in 2005
Edition 2026

ISBN-10: 81-7479-069-1
ISBN-13: 978-81-7479-069-9

Published by
Kaveri Books
4832/24, Ansari Road
New Delhi-110002 (India)
Tel: 011- 4707 2321
E-mail : info@kaveribooks.com
kaveribooks@gmail.com
website: www.kaveribooks.com

PRINTED IN INDIA

Preface

Terrorism is a formidable morass. What we have endured so far is nothing what remains in store is absolutely purifying. Inspite of having killed thousands of terrorists and arrested several times more, we are still nowhere near controlling terrorism that defies a political police or military solution.

Unlike the weather, however terrorism is something that we have far greater power to do something about. Unfortunately despite the fact that the Indian state has been facing insurgencies and terrorism of various intensities almost since the moment of its birth, it has failed to systematize its approach to the problem, to document its past policies and their consequences and to learn from the vast but presently dispersed, funds of experiences that have been generated.

Over the past decades, terrorist movements have emerged in state after state in India. Our responses unfortunately, have remained trapped in the same senseless cycle as disaster follows disaster.

At the very heart of the problem is the question of defining a coherent and comprehensive policy framework on internal security.

The very first imperative of an effective policy on internal security, consequently, requires the definition of the basic principles on which all action and policy are to be constructed. We are yet to set up systematic defences against the far greater threats have already been realised, and are currently undermining the rule of law and even the possibility of civil governance in may parts of the country.

In view of the future threat potential of low intensity wars it is crucial that a radical reformation of internal security forces be initiated creating skills, knowledge, attitudes and infrastructure necessary to confront this danger and possibly raising entirely new forces to grapple with this specific hazard.

I shall regard my efforts amply rewarded if the book is received with the enthusiasm by the readers.

I wish to express my sincere thanks to Mr. Rakesh Goel of Kaveri Books, for their continued interest in bringing out this edition.

H. Parameshwar Hegde

Contents

1

Meaning of Terrorism

Introduction

Terrorism is simply one of the several tools employed by the insurgents. The secret of the success of the terrorists lies in the fact that they are able to create a climate of fear, panic, disorientation and capitulation out of all proportion to the actual military strength of their group and the popular support to it. They judge their success in terms of the political, psychological and propaganda impact of their actions rather than the traditional military criteria of casualties inflicted and damage caused. Thus terrorism is a particularly potent tool against soft states, against regimes which lack resolve, and states which lack the moral courage to admit some of the harsh unpalatable realities built in their socio-political system. Since unlike most of the countries of Europe and some of Asia which have gone through a horrific amount of human suffering and bloodshed in the wars of the twentieth century, this country has not had its due share of it, the Indian society has developed a morbid fear of violence. Consequently, as the recent examples of capitulation before the terrorists also show, intelligent terrorists can certainly extort far more out of the Indian nation state than they can ever expect from a principled and resolute state. In India, this is one of the reasons that most insurgent movements keep on resorting to acts of terrorism even when they are militarily capable of continuing the guerrilla warfare stage.

Terrorist inspired by the communist ideology present a classic case of anachronism both in time and place. As far as time is concerned, the ideology is very much *passe;* as far as place is concerned, the ideology is very much against the grain of the collective Indian psyche. That the left-wing violence has never been able to elevate itself beyond the level of terrorism despite its 33 years of existence must be regarded as proof of the inherent weaknesses of the movement; however, that it has not yet been possible to eradicate it must be regarded as a proof of the inherent weaknesses of the police response in dealing with it. Presently, the focus of violence is on Andhra Pradesh, followed by Bihar. The disturbing possibility in this connection is that the PWG and the MCC could forage links with the LTTE, the North-Eastern insurgents and the Maoist insurgents of Nepal–the nexus could qualitatively change the nature of violence.

The word 'terrorism' was first popularized during the French Revolution. In contrast to its contemporary usage, at that time terrorism had a decidedly *positive* connotation. The system or *régime de la terreur* of 1793-94 from which the English word came–was adopted as a means to establish order during the transient anarchical period of turmoil and upheaval that followed the uprisings of 1789, as it has followed in the wake of many other revolutions. Hence, unlike terrorism as it is commonly understood today, to mean a *révolutionary* or anti-government activity undertaken by non-state or subnational entities, the *régime de la terreur* was an instrument of governance wielded by the recently established revolutionary *state.* It was designed to consolidate the new government's power by intimidating counter-revolutionaries, subversives and all other dissidents whom the new regime regarded as 'enemies of the people.' The Committee of General Security and the Revolutionary Tribunal ('People's Court' in the modern vernacular) were thus accorded wide powers of arrest and judgement, publicly putting to death by guillotine persons convicted of treasonous (*i.e.*, reactionary) crimes. In this manner, a powerful lesson was conveyed to any and all who might oppose the revolution or grow nostalgic for the *ancien régime.*

Ironically, perhaps, terrorism in its original context was also closely associated with the ideas of virtue and democracy. The revolutionary leader Maximilien Robespierre firmly believed that virtue was the mainspring of a popular government at peace, but that during the time of revolution must be allied with terror in order for democracy to triumph. He appealed famously to 'virtue, without which terror is evil; terror, without which virtue is helpless,' and proclaimed; 'Terror is nothing but justice, prompt, severe and inflexible; it is therefore an emanation of virtue.'

Terrorism, in the most widely accepted contemporary usage of the term, is fundamentally and inherently political. It is also ineluctably about power: the pursuit of power, the acquisition of power, and the use of power to achieve political change. Terrorism is thus violence–or, equally important, the threat of violence–used and directed in pursuit of, or in service of, a political aim. With this vital point clearly illuminated, one can appreciate the significance of the additional definition of 'terrorist' provided by the *OED*: 'Anyone who attempts to further his views by a system of coercive intimidation.' This definition underscores clearly the other fundamental characteristics of terrorism: that it is a planned, calculated, and indeed systematic act.

Problems in Different States

The insurgents are taking full advantage of the porosity of the border in having a free run. Many of them are deeply involved in narcotics smuggling also. Presently, though there is a ceasefire in effect, it remains to be seen whether we will be able to arrive at an honourable agreement that would be acceptable to the neighbouring states also.

Insurgency in Tripura is born of the ethno-economic conflict between the tribals and the non-tribals. This is one movement where the element of communal hatred is very strong. About a score of terrorist outfits are now operating in Tripura. It has been widely alleged that the political parties have actually preferred to profit by making secret use of the forces of the various insurgent outfits in furtherance of their vested political interests and against their opponents. In this process, a criminalisation of the movement was deliberately encouraged. Thus a vicious circle has been established that is permitting a continuation of insurgent activities.

Insurgency in Manipur is a rather unique case–it is not as much innate as it is acquired from exposure to the insurgent movements all around the state. The Manipuri youth had no specific grievance to base their movement on. At best it was the failure of the political system in delivering the expected results. There was, of course, the additional dimension of demographic complexities. All this has resulted in a confusing picture of violence featuring attacks on security forces, inter-group clashes and ethnic strife. Regarding the Kuki-Naga clashes there have once again been allegations of the Kukis receiving support from a certain section of politicians in more than one state.

Peace has returned to Mizoram after two decades of violence from 1966 to 1986. But the Mizoram border is still being freely used by insurgents of other states. Mizo insurgency had also lacked any sound ideological basis or even a viable *locus standi*. Peace was virtually purchased through some far from honourable methods of political expedience. In any case, there is no reason to believe that the methods which worked with Lal Denga will necessarily work with others too.

Though the media and the intelligence agencies have indulged in a great deal of hyperbole, the fact remains that the Indian insurgents do not possess anything very sophisticated in their armament, and certainly not anything better than those possessed by the security forces. The media has, of course, pure sensationalism in mind where a single hand grenade is described as capable of blowing up a three-storeyed building; the intelligence agencies and the forces have a very despicable tendency of ascribing the most devastating weaponry to the insurgents so that they could cover their own incompetence. Further, an analysis of the pattern of attacks by the insurgents shows that they have been going about their business in a highly unprofessional manner–the execution of the ornate designs of the ISI is certainly not as elegant as they would have loved it to be. However, there is no reason to indulge in the wishful thinking that the incompetence of the government agencies would always be matched by the clumsiness of the insurgents. The Government would be in for a singularly rude shock when they encounter professionally competent terrorists.

The very fact that in spite of having killed and arrested thousands of insurgents in various parts of the country over the years we have not at all been able to cleanse our system of its insurrectionary tendencies shows that there is something very fundamentally wrong with our approach to counterinsurgency operations. Myopic as we are, we have persistently refused to admit that an insurgency is primarily a socio-political phenomenon, and only secondarily a police problem. It is not possible to successfully counterinsurgencies without understanding their true nature. Insurgencies are qualitatively different from the usual law and order problems or public order problems. Various manifestations of the insurgencies may be reminiscent of well-known law and order or public order problems; but they still demand an altogether different treatment. Instead of responding to each incident individually, as we generally do, we must develop a comprehensive strategy for counterinsurgency. We have already seen that no government is ever likely to possess enough resources to extinguish all the fires and prevent new ones at the same time. Thus a regime that is given to seeking *ad hoc* solutions or one that is used to mere fire-fighting is doing nothing but writing a sure recipe for inevitable disaster.

The Punjab problem is a classic reminder of the fact that appeasement is the road to war. The impuissance which was shown in the 1950s before the religio-linguistic politics of the Akali Dal was to ultimately result in the spectre of terrorism in the 1980s. It should not come as a surprise that the terrorists used the Anandpur Sahib resolutions to derive some sort of theoretical validity for their demand of Khalistan. Terrorism could flourish in Punjab simply because in the early years the response of the administration was utterly irresolute. Bhindranwale was, in a way, allowed to grow; the most ignominious way in which he was unconditionally released from custody less than a month after his arrest on murder charges catapulted him almost overnight to the status of a great leader. Eventually the cathartic option of Operation Blue Star had to be exercised. That was a limited tactical success, but extremely costly in many other aspects. The instances of Major Gen. Subeg Singh, S.S. Mann, DIG and the revolt in several Sikh Units of the Indian army underscored the unsavoury fact that in a nascent nation state like ours in which we are obliged to infuse the spirit of nationalism almost everyday through all sorts of contrived means, parochial loyalties are always capable of overriding national loyalties. In any case, terrorism in Punjab was brought under control once the administration resolved to shake off the demoralisation, subversion and lethargy that had set in among the ranks. It should also be kept in mind that the demand for Khalistan was never a popular movement; the masses never lost sight of the fact that given the dispersal of the Sikh community all over the country, their interests, economic or otherwise, were inextricably linked with the rest of the country. Sikh terrorism now survives as a sporadic phenomenon wholly supported and sustained by their wealthy sympathisers abroad. They have the capacity to justify their existence by some sensational strikes.

Assam is yet another example where the politics of parochialism has eventually led to ISI supported secessionist violence. No affront could be more serious for the nation than the insolent way in which the ULFA keeps on killing the non-Assamese people. In Assam also, the parochial movement claiming its base in the relative deprivation of the native Assamese people was never a popular one. However, the elite classes which pursued it, did so it with such dexterity that they ultimately grabbed political power through it. It is rather distressing irony of fate that the ULFA came to be created by some of their estranged comrades-in-arms only. The ULFA is not suspected of having very strong links with not only the ISI but also with other important outfits of the neighbouring states like the NSCN.

Nagaland is one place where, in the course of fourty-five years, we have allowed the insurgents to progress from their primitive spears to modern machine guns. Naga insurgency is essentially an ethnic-cum-racial problem and the rumbling of a discordant note were heard even during the British period. Though we had been able to engineer the Shillong Accord, Naga insurgency is being run successfully from across the border in Myanmar.

The origin of many of the fissiparous tendencies in the body politic of this country may be traced to its unique socio-political legacy and history. Insurgent situations in the Indian context are essentially virulent manifestations of the identity crises of various small constituent groups vis-à-vis the large ensuing group, that is, the nation state. These identity crises could be based on ethnicity, race, religion, language or any other factor. Some groups might argue that nations are created by consensus and their consent was not involved in the original process of nation building, or that the process itself was farcical. In other words, we are facing insurgencies because some of the constituents of the nation have developed incongruities with respect to the unifying principles of nationalism. Theoretically one could think of several grounds for such incongruities. In practice, however, we find that most of the Indian insurgents have not bothered to develop a rational ideological framework for themselves. At an ideological level they remain nothing but some *ad-hoc* melange of convenient, attractive and irrational notions.

Growth of Terrorism

On the eve of the First World War, terrorism still retained its revolutionary connotations. By this time, growing unrest and irrendentist ferment had already welled up within the decaying Ottoman and Habsburg Empires. In the 1880s and 1890s, for example, militant Armenian nationalist movements in eastern Turkey pursued a terrorist strategy against continued Ottoman rule of a kind that would later be adopted by most of the post–Second World War ethno-nationalist/separatist movements. The Armenians objective was simultaneously to strike a blow against the despotic 'alien' regime through repeated attacks on its colonial administration and security forces, in order to rally indigenous support, as well as to attract international attention, sympathy and support. Around the same time, the Inner Macedonian Revolutionary Organization (IMRO) was active in the region overlapping present-day Greece, Bulgaria and Serbia. Although the Macedonians did not go on to suffer the catastrophic fate that befell the Armenians during the First World War (when an estimated one million persons perished in what is considered to be the first officially implemented genocide of the twentieth century), IMRO never came close to achieving its aim of an independent Macedonia and thereafter degenerated into a mostly criminal organization of hired thugs and political assassins.

The events immediately preceding the First World War in Bosnia are of course more familiar because of their subsequent cataclysmic impact on world affairs. There, similar groups of disaffected nationalists–Bosnian Serb intellectuals, university, students and even schoolchildren, collectively known as Mlada Bosna, or Young Bosnians–arose against continued Habsburg suzerainty.

While it is perhaps easy to dismiss the movement, as some historians have, as comprised of 'frustrated, poor, dreary and maladjusted' adolescents–much as many contemporary observers similarly denigrate modem-day terrorists as mindless, obsessive and maladjusted–it was a member of Young Bosnia, Gavrilo Princip, who is widely credited with having set in motion the chain of events that began on 28th June 1914, when he assassinated the Habsburg Archduke Franz Ferdinand in Sarajevo, and culminated in the first World War. Whatever its superficially juvenile characteristics, the group was nonetheless passionately dedicated to the attainment of a federal South Slav political entity–uniting Slovenes, Croats and Serbs–and resolutely committed to assassination as the vehicle with which to achieve that aim. In this respect, the Young Bosnians perhaps had more in common with the radical republicanism of Giuseppe Mazzini, one the most ardent exponent of Italian unification in the nineteenth century, than with groups such as the Narodnaya Volya–despite a shared conviction in the efficacy of tyrannicide. An even more significant difference, however, was the degree of involvement in, and external support provided to, Young Bosnian activities by various shadowy Serbian nationalist groups. Principal among these was the Pan-Serb Secret Society, the Narodna Obrana ('The People's Defence' or 'National Defence').

By the 1930s, the meaning of 'terrorism' had changed again. It was now used less to refer to revolutionary movements and violence directed against governments and their leaders, and more to describe the practices of mass repression employed by totalitarian states and their dictatorial leaders against their own citizens. Thus, the term regained its former connotations of abuse of power by governments, and was applied specificially to the authoritarian regimes that had come to power in Fascist Italy, Nazi Germany and Stalinist Russia. In Germany and Italy respectively, the accession to office of Hitler and Mussolini had depended in large measure on the 'street'–the mobilization and deployment of gangs of brown–or black-shirted thugs to harass and intimidate political opponents and root out other scapegoats for public vilification and further victimization. 'Terror Never,' Mussolini insisted, demurely dismissing such intimidation as 'simply...social hygiene, taking those individuals out of circulation like a doctor would take out a bacillus.' The most sinister dimension of this form of 'terror' was that it became an intrinsic component of Fascist and Nazi governance, executed at the behest of, and in complete subservience to, the ruling political party of the land–which had arrogated to itself complete, total control of the country and its people. A system of government sanctioned fear and coercion was thus created whereby political brawls, street fights and widespread persecution of Jews, communists and other declared 'enemies of the state' became the means through which complete and submissive compliance was ensured.

The 'Great Terror' that Stalin was shortly to unleash in Russia both resembled and differed from that of the Nazis. On the one hand, drawing inspiration from Hitler's ruthless elimination of his own political opponents, the Russian dictator similarly transformed the political party he led into a servile instrument responsive directly to his personal will, and the state's police and security apparatus into slavish organs of coercion, enforcement and repression. But conditions in the Soviet Union of the 1930s more little resemblance to the turbulent political, social and economic upheaval afflicting Germany and Italy during that decade and the previous one. On the other hand, therefore, unlike either the Nazis or the Fascists, who had emerged from the political free-for-alls in their own countries to seize power and then had to struggle to consolidate their rule and retain their unchallenged authority the Russian Communist Party had by the mid-1930s been firmly entrenched in power for more than a decade.

Following the Second World War, in another swing of the pendulum of meaning, 'terrorism' regained the revolutionary connotations with which it is most commonly associated today. At that time, the term was used primarily in reference to the violent revolts then being prosecuted by the various indigenous nationalist/ anti-colonialist groups that emerged in Asia, Africa and the Middle East during the late 1940s and 1950s to oppose continued European rule. Countries as diverse as Israel, Kenya, Cyprus and Algeria for example, owe their independence at least in part to nationalist political movements that employed terrorism against colonial powers. It was also during this period that the 'politically correct' appellation of 'freedom fighters' came into fashion as a result of the political legitimacy that the international community (whose sympathy and support was actively courted by many of these movements) accorded to struggles for national liberation and self-determination. Many newly independent Third World countries and communist bloc states in particular adopted this vernacular, arguing that anyone or any movement that fought against 'colonial' oppression and/or Western domination should not be described as 'terrorists,' but were properly deemed to be 'freedom fighters.' This position was perhaps most famously explained by the Palestine

Liberation Organization (PLO) Chairman Yassir Arafat, when he addressed the United Nations General Assembly in November 1974; 'The difference between the revolutionary and the terrorist,' Arafat stated, 'lies in the reason for which each fights. For whoever stands by a just cause and fights for the freedom and liberation of his and from the invaders, the settlers and the colonialists, cannot possibly be called terrorist….'

During the late 1960s and 1970s, terrorism continued to be viewed within a revolutionary context. However, this usage now expanded to include nationalist and ethnic separatist groups outside a colonial or neo-colonial framework as well as radical, entirely ideologically motivated organizations. Disenfranchise or exiled nationalist minorities–such as the PLO, the Quebecois separatist group FLQ (Front de Liberation du Québec), the Basque ETA (Euskadi ta Askatasuna, or Freedom for the Basque Homeland) and even a hitherto unknown South Moluccan irredentist group seeking independence from Indonesia adopted terrorism as a means to draw attention to themselves and their respective causes, in many instances with the specific aim, like their anti-colonial predecessors, of attracting international sympathy and support. Around the same time, various left-wing political extremists drawn mostly from the radical student organizations and Marxist/Leninist/Maoist movements in Western Europe, Latin America and the United States–began to form terrorist groups opposing American intervention in Vietnam and what they claimed were the irredeemable social and economic inequities of the modem capitalist liberal-democratic state.

Although the revolutionary cum ethno-nationalist/separatist and ideological exemplars continue to shape our most basic understanding of the term, in recent years 'terrorism' has been used to denote broader, less distinct phenomena. In the early 1980s, for example, terrorism came to be regarded as a calculated means to destabilize the West as part of a vast global conspiracy. Books like *The Terror Network* by Claire Sterling propagated the notion to a receptive American presidential administration and similarly susceptible governments elsewhere that the seemingly isolated terrorist incidents perpetrated by disparate groups scattered across the globe were in fact linked elements of a massive clandestine plot, orchestrated by the Kremlin and implemented by its Warsaw Pact client states, to destroy the Free World.

In the early 1990s the meaning and usage of the term 'terrorism' were further blurred by the emergence of two new buzzwords: 'narco-terrorism' and the so-called 'gray area phenomenon.' The former term revived the Mosocw-orchestrated terrorism conspiracy theories of previous years while introducing the critical new dimension of narcotics trafficking. Thus, 'narco-terrorism' was defined by one of the concept's foremost propagators as the 'use of drug trafficking to advance the objectives of certain governments and terrorist organizations'–identified as the 'Marxist-Leninist regimes' of the Soviet Union, Cuba, Bulgaria and Nicaragua, among others. The emphasis on 'narco-terrorism' as the latest manifestation of the communist plot to undermine Western society, however, had the unfortunate effect of diverting official attention away from a bonafide emerging trend. To a greater extent than ever in the past, entirely criminal (that is, violent, *economically* motivated) organizations were now forging strategic alliances with terrorist and guerrilla organizations or themselves employing violence for specifically political ends. The growing power of the Colombian cocaine cartels, their close ties with left-wing terrorist groups in Colombia and Peru, and their repeated attempts to subvert Colombia's electoral process and undermine successive governments constitute perhaps the best-known example of this continuing trend.

Terrorist as a Citizen

What all these examples suggest is that terrorists clearly do not see or regard themselves as others do. Above all I am a family man,' the archterrorist Carlos, 'The jackal,' described himself to a French newspaper following his capture in 1994. Cast perpetually on the defensive and forced to take up arms to protect themselves and their real or imagined constituents only, terrorists perceive themselves as reluctant warriors, driven by desperation-and lacking any viable alternative-to violence against a repressive state, a predatory rival ethnic or nationalist group, or an unresponsive international order. This perceived characteristic of self-denial also distinguishes the terrorist from other types of political extremists as well as from persons similarly involved in illegal, violent avocations. A communist or a revolutionary, for example, would likely readily accept and admit that he is in fact a communist or a revolutionary. Indeed, many would doubtless take particular pride in claiming either of those appellations for themselves. Similarly, even a person engaged in illegal, wholly disreputable or entirely selfish violent activities, such as robbing banks or carrying out contract killings, would probably admit to being a bank robber or a murderer for hire. The terrorist, by contrast, will *never* acknowledge that he is a terrorist and moreover will go to great lengths to evade and obscure any such inference or connection. Terry Anderson, the American journalist who was held hostage for almost seven years by the Lebanese terrorist organization Hezbollah, relates a telling conversation he had with one of his guards. The guard had objected to a newspaper article that referred to Hezbollah as terrorists. 'We are not terrorists,' he indignantly stated, 'we are fighters.' Anderson replied, 'Hajj, you are a terrorist, look it up in the dictionary. You are a terrorist, you may not like the word and if you do not like the word, do not do it.

The terrorist will always argue that it is society or the government or the socio-economic 'system' and its laws that are the *real* 'terrorists,' and moreover that if it were not for this oppression, he would not have felt the need to defend either himself or the population he claims to represent. Another revealing example of this process of obfuscation-projection may be found in the book *Invisible Armies,* written by Sheikh Muhammad Hussein Fadlallah, the spiritual leader of the Lebanese terrorist group responsible for Anderson's kidnapping. 'We don't see ourselves as terrorist,' Fadlallah explains, 'because we don't believe in terrorism. We don't see resisting the occupier as a terrorist action.

Terrorism is a pejorative term. It is a word with intrinsically negative connotations that is generally applied to one's enemies and opponents, or to those with whom one disagrees and would otherwise prefer to ignore. 'What is called terrorism,' Brian Jenkins has written, 'thus seems to depend on one's point of view. Use of the term implies a moral judgement; and if one party can successfully attach the label *terrorist* to its opponent, then it has indirectly persuaded others to adopt its moral viewpoint.' Hence, the decision to call someone or label some organization 'terrorist' becomes almost unavoidably subjective, depending largely on whether one sympathizes with or opposes the person group cause concerned. If one identifies with the victim of the violence, for example, then the act is terrorism. If, however, one identifies with the perpetrator, the violent act is regarded in a more sympathetic, if not positive (or, at the worst, an ambivalent) light; and it is not terrorism.

Terrorists, as we have seen, deliberately cloak themselves in the terminology of military jargon. They consciously portray themselves as bonafide (freedom) fighters, if not soldiers, who–though they wear no identifying uniform or insignia–are entitled to treatment as prisoners of war (POWs) if captured and therefore should not be prosecuted as common criminals in ordinary courts of law. Terrorists further argue that, because of their numerical inferiority, far more limited firepower and paucity of resources compared with an established nation-state's massive defence and national security apparatus, they have no choice but to operate clandestinely, emerging from the shadows to carry out dramatic (in other words, bloody and destructive) acts of hit-and-run violence in order to attract attention to, and ensure publicity for, themselves and their cause. The bomb-in-the-rubbish-bin, in their view, is merely a circumstantially imposed 'poor man's air force': the only means with which the terrorist can challenge–and get the attention of–the more powerful state.

Definition of Terrorism

The US Federal Bureau of Investigation (FBI) defines terrorism as follows:

> The unlawful use of force or violence against persons or property to intimidate or coerce a Government, the civilian population, or any segment thereof, in furtherance of political or social objectives,

and the US Department of Defense defines it as

> The unlawful use of–or threatened use of–force or violence against individuals or property to coerce or intimidate governments or societies, often to achieve political, religious, or ideological objectives.

Not surprisingly, each of the above definitions reflects the priorities and particular interests of the specific agency involved. The State Department's emphasis is on the premeditated and planned or calculated nature of terrorism in contrast to more spontaneous acts of political violence. Its definition is also the only one of the three to emphasize both the ineluctably political nature of terrorism and the perpetrators' fundamental 'subnational' characteristic. The State Department definition, however, is conspicuously deficient in failing to consider the psychological dimension of terrorism. Terrorism is as much about the threat of violence as the violent act itself and, accordingly, is deliberately conceived to have far-reaching psychological repercussions beyond the actual target of the act among a wider, watching, 'target' audience. As Jenkins succinctly observed, 'Terrorism is theatre.'

Given the FBI's mission of investigating and solving crimes–both political (*e.g.* terrorism) and other–it is not surprising that its definition focuses on different elements. Unlike the State Department, this definition does address the psychological dimensions of the terrorist act described above, laying stress on terrorism's intimidatory and coercive aspects. The FBI definition also identifies a much broader category of terrorists targets than only 'non-combinants,' specifying not only governments and their citizens, but also inanimate objects, such as private and public property. The FBI definition further recognizes social alongside political objects as fundamental terrorist aims–though it offers no clearer elucidation of either.

The Department of Defence definition of terrorism is arguably the most complete of the three. It highlights the terrorist threat as much as the actual act of violence and focuses on terrorism's targeting of whole societies as well as governments. The Defence Department definition further cites the religious and ideological aims of terrorism alongside its fundamental political objectives–but curiously omits the social dimension found in the FBI's definition.

It is not only individual agencies within the same governmental apparatus that cannot agree on a single definition of terrorism. Experts and other long-established scholars in the field are equally incapable of reaching a consensus. In the first edition of his magisterial survey, *Political Terrrorism: A Research Guide,* Alex Schmid devoted more than a hundred pages to examining more than a hundred different definitions of terrorism in an effort to discover a broadly acceptable, reasonably comprehensive explication of the word. Four years and a second edition later, Schmid was no closer to the goal of his quest, conceding in the first sentence of the revised volume that the 'search for an adequate definition is still on.' Walter Laqueur despaired of defining terrorism in both editions of his monumental work on the subject, maintaining that it is neither possible to do so nor worthwhile to make the attempt. 'Ten years of debates on typologies and definitions,' he responded to a survey on definitions conducted by Schmid, 'have not enhanced our knowledge of the subject to a significant degree.' Laqueur's contention is supported by the twenty-two different word categories occurring in the 109 different definitions that Schmid identified in his survey. Terrorism is often confused or equated with, or treated as synonymous with, guerrilla warfare. This is not entirely surprising, since guerrillas often employ the same tactics (assassination, kidnapping, bombings of public gathering-places, hostage-taking, etc.) for the same purposes (to intimidate or coerce, thereby affecting behaviour through the arousal of fear) as terrorists. In addition, both terrorists and guerrillas wear neither uniform nor identifying insignia and thus are often indistinguishable from non-combatants. However, despite the inclination to lump both terrorists and guerrillas into the same catch-all category of 'irregulars,' there are nonetheless fundamental differences between the two. 'Guerrilla,' for example, in its most widely accepted usage, is taken to refer to a numerically larger group of armed individuals, who operate as a military unit, attack enemy military forces, and seize and hold territory (even if only ephemerally during daylight hours), while also exercising some form of sovereignty or control over a defined geographical area and its population. Terrorists, however, do not function in the open as armed units, generally do not attempt to seize or hold territory, deliberately avoid engaging enemy military forces in combat and rarely exercise any direct control or sovereignty either over territory or population.

It is also useful to distinguish terrorists from ordinary criminals. Like terrorists, criminals use violence as a means to attaining a specific end. However, while the violent act itself may be similar–kidnapping, shooting, arson, for example–the purpose or motivation clearly is not. Whether the criminal employs violence as a means to obtain money, to acquire material goods, or to kill or injure a specific victim for pay, he is acting primarily for selfish, personal motivations (usually material gain). Moreover, unlike terrorism, the ordinary criminal's violent act is not designed or intended to have consequences or create psychological repercussions beyond the act itself. The criminal may of course use some short-term act of violence to 'terrorize' his victim, such as waving a gun in the face of bank clerk during a robbery in order to ensure the clerk's expeditious compliance. In these instances, however, the bank robber is conveying no 'message' (political or otherwise) through his act of violence beyond facilitating the rapid handing over of his 'loot.' The criminal's act therefore is not meant to have any effect reaching beyond either the incident itself or the immediate victim. Further, the violence is neither conceived nor intended to convey any message to anyone other than the bank clerk himself, whose rapid co-operation is the robber's only objective. Perhaps most fundamentally, the criminal is not concerned with influencing or affecting public opinion: he simply wants to abscond with his money or accomplish his mercenary task in the quickest and easiest way possible so that he may reap his reward and enjoy the fruits of his labours. By contrast, the fundamental aim of the terrorist's violence is ultimately to change 'the system'–about which the ordinary criminal, of course, couldn't care less.

The Nature of a Terrorist

The terrorist is also very different from the lunatic assassin, who may use identical tactics (*e.g.*, shooting, bombing) and perhaps even seeks the same objective (*e.g.*, the death of a political figure). However, while the tactics and targets of terrorists and lone assassins are often identical, their purpose is not. Whereas the terrorist's goal is again ineluctably *political* (to change or fundamentally alter a political system through his violent act), the lunatic assassin's goal is more often intrinsically idiosyncratic, completely egocentric and deeply personal. John Hinckley, who tried to kill President Reagan in 1981 to impress the actress Jodie Foster, is a case in point. He acted not from political motivation or ideological conviction but to fulfil some profound personal quest (killing the president to impress his screen idol). Such unlike the ordinary criminal or the lunatic assassin, the terrorist is not pursuing purely egocentric goals–he is not driven by the wish to line his own pocket or satisfy some personal need or grievance. The terrorist is fundamentally an *altruist:* he believes that he is serving a 'good' cause designed to achieve a greater good for a wider constituency–whether real or imagined–which the terrorist and his organization purport to represent. The criminal, by comparison, serves no cause at all, just his own personal aggrandizement and material satiation. Indeed, a 'terrorist without a cause (at least in his own mind),' Konrad Kellen has argued, 'is not a terrorist.' Yet the possession or identification of a cause is not a sufficient criterion for labelling someone a terrorist. In this key respect, the difference between terrorists and political extremists is clear. Many persons, of course, harbour all sorts of radical and extreme beliefs and opinions, and many of them belong to radical or even illegal or proscribed political organizations. However, if they do not use violence in the pursuance of their beliefs, they cannot be considered terrorists. The terrorist is fundamentally a *violent intellectual,* prepared to use and indeed committed to using force in the attainment of his goals.

2

Characteristics of Terrorism and Insurgency

Terrorism as a Phenomenon

We are all aware of terrorism as a phenomenon in the contemporary world, but we are less precise about what events deserve that highly perjorative label 'terrorist.' There is no universally accepted definition of terrorism, although a number of formulations are widely used. Two in particular seem to this writer to illuminate the essential elements of terrorism and provide some basic pointers for decision makers. The first defines terrorism as 'a symbolic act designed to influence political behaviour by extranormal means entailing the use or threat of violence.' The second asserts that terrorism is the 'threat or use of violence for political purposes, when such action is intended to influence the attitude and behaviour of a target group other than its immediate victims and its ramifications transcend national boundaries. Both take as their starting point the fact that terrorism is violent political activity. There is no terrorism without violence and coercion. There is no terrorism in the absence of political motivation. In fact, as Lenin might have observed, terrorism is the continuation of politics by violent means.

However, not all violent political acts are intrinsically terrorist, as one can see from the many national liberation struggles of the post-War World. In order to have acts of international terrorism, additional elements are needed. The two definitions provide those elements–the concept of extranormality and the transcending of national boundaries. Terrorism is abnormal because it almost always chooses as targets and as weapons innocent non-combatant diplomats in an embassy, passengers on an airplane or tram, students on a bus, or businessmen kidnapped for ransom. These targets are non-military, frequently with no direct connection to the cause being promoted. The victims are used cynically as the tools whereby public attention can be focused on a political cause and a wider international audience can be influenced. Terrorism can also be considered abnormal when certain kinds of acts are involved: hijacking, hostage taking, kidnapping, letter-bombing. Under international law, all are regarded as illegitimate, inhumane, and unjustifiable acts of violence.

Insurgency can be defined as a struggle between a non-ruling group and the ruling authorities in which the former consciously employs political resources (organisational skills, propaganda and/ or demonstrations) and instruments of (ostensibly illegal) violence to establish legitimacy for some aspect of the political system it considers illegitimate. Thus an insurgency is an exertion in open resistance against a constitutional government or established authority which falls short of a revolution or civil war. A belligerent involved in activities having an insurrectionary focus becomes an insurgent. It is important to note that the emphasis is on 'open resistance' or 'defiance' of the authority, and its falling short of a revolution or civil war. If the rebellion succeeds, it becomes a revolution meaning that the insurgency is over–from an opposition to authority it becomes the authority itself. One man's insurgent could easily be another man's freedom fighter.

The central idea is thus found to be the defiance of, and an attempt to undermine the authority of, a larger group by a smaller group. Most commonly the larger group is a nation state. It should, therefore, be desirable to have a brief overview of the theories of nation states and nationalism so that we may see as to how the absence of or the anomalies in respect of one or more of the essential ingredients provide a theoretical ground for an insurgency to take roots. The object of the following study is to define the pillars of the nation states and, by extension, those of nationalism so that we may perceive the constituents of the so-called 'anti-national' syllogism.

The terrorist is espousing a particular political cause. His targets, immediate and ultimate, are carefully chosen. A particular outcome–publicity, ransom, prisoner release–is clearly defined. Our response therefore must be equally well-tailored to the specific means and tactics of each group which sponsors and espouses terrorism.

The distinction between ends and means is at the heart of any policy and decision-making process related to terrorism. We are all aware of the diversity of causes to which terrorists appeal. Some groups, such as the Baader-Meinhof Gang and its successors, the Italian Red and the Japanese Red Army, Brigades seek the total overthrow of the capitalist system. Others demand merely a change in regime or a transition to majority rule, as in Central America and Southern Africa. Yet others pursue nationalist or ethnocentric goals–a united Ireland, a homeland for the Palestinians, a Baseque Carotian or South Moluccan state. Some of these causes, such as majority rule in Southern Africa, we can actively support. Many others provoke passionate and emotional debate. Yet all these groups have been characterized as terrorist from one perspective or another, and all have carried out individual acts of hostage taking or terrorist violence which have been generally condemned. It is not easy to devise a global policy for combating terrorism as long as we focus only on the terrorist's goals and objectives. We also must consider the means they employ.

Similarly, with respect to terrorism, we have been working to differentiate between those political activities which are legitimate and those which deserve universal condemnation. The predisposition of the terrorist to use innocent civilians as the instruments of his purpose is particularly disturbing. Hijacking of planes, kidnapping, and the taking of hostages are increasingly recognized by the international community as contrary to a basic moral standard. The willingness of the United Nations to draft and promote conventions against hijacking, aircraft sabotage, attacks on diplomats, and hostage taking is evidence of this growing awareness. There is also increasing condemnation of the use of certain weapon systems-surface-to-air missiles and rocket launchers-when these are directed at non-military targets, or nuclear, biological, and chemical agents irrespective of target. The basic strategy of the United States has been to seek to broaden this international consensus to include as wide a spectrum of acts as possible, while at the same time seeking, whenever feasible, to remove terrorism's underlying causes.

Even if we have clarified our thinking about the nature of a terrorist act and its relationship to certain political goals, we still must define a coherent government policy to respond to terrorist violence. Such a policy must come to grips with the fundamental issues of whether and under what circumstances concessions should be made to terrorist demands, when and how negotiations should be conducted, and according to what rules military force can be used. The US Government repeatedly has stated its view that it will not pay ransom and will not release prisoners in order to achieve the release of hostages. We look to foreign governments to assume responsibility for resolving all such situations. We do not, however, refuse to negotiate with or to talk to the terrorists. We believe that dialogue is an essential element of any strategy, even though it may be limited to a discussion of the provision of food and water and other humanitarian concerns.

Purpose of the Working Group

Beginning in 1972 after the Lod Airport and Munich Olympic Games massacres, the US Government recognized a need to deal with terrorism on more than an *ad-hoc* basis. At that time, the President created a Cabinet Committee and a Working Group on Terrorism subordinate to it. The former was abolished in 1977, having met only once, while the Working Group was placed under the National Security Council's Special Co-ordination Committee, a Cabinet-level body charged specifically with responsibility for both policy and crisis management issues. The Working Group has over thirty members, primarily federal agencies with law enforcement, intelligence or operational responsibilities in the field of terrorism. It is a large and unwieldy group with disparate interests. In order to focus more precisely on matters of major concern, the Working Group has been broken down into several smaller units: an Executive Committee charged with reviewing major policy and crisis management issues and a number of sub-committees responsible for functional problems of concern to only a limited number of member agencies. These functional areas include research and development, physical security, contingency planning, public affairs, and international initiatives.

The principal purpose of the Working Group is to ensure prompt and effective inter-agency coordination, which is often lacking in the vast federal bureaucracy. Until recently, however, it has not attempted to address the more complex, and in the domestic area more important, area of vertical coordination: the linkages between the federal government and state and local authorities. As the events at Three-Mile Island demonstrated in a different context, we need to be able to respond to crises and disasters very quickly and in ways that ensure close co-operation between all affected jurisdictions. When domestic terrorist incidents occur, local law enforcement authorities are often the first on the scene, even in crimes which involve federal jurisdiction. It is essential that they have close working relationships with the FBI and other federal agencies charged with handling such incidents. Since local authorities often have responsibility for preventive measures, there is also a critical need to share intelligence on terrorist groups and plans. Unfortunately, such an exchange sometimes is limited by the lack of national security clearances at the local level.

The Working Group is attempting to address the vertical coordination problem in two ways. We have invited representative of the National Governors Association and the National League of Cities to take part in our activities. These two organizations provide critical links to the governors and mayors and to those on their respective staffs concerned with emergency planning and crisis management. We are also encouraging and in some cases funding exercises, games, and scenarios designed to test interactions between the federal system and state and local authorities.

Much progress in the area of co-ordination has already been made; much more is possible. Nonetheless, a group of thirty agencies, even if a close working relationship among the members exists, is not the ideal body for incident management. When a terrorist act occurs, we have found that it is desirable to concentrate and focus responsibility in one lead agency. There are three agencies with lead responsibility: the Department of State for all terrorist incidents outside the United States involving American interests; the 'FBI for incidents inside the United States; and the Federal Aviation Administration for hijackings in American jurisdiction. Each of these agencies has a modern crisis centre from which contact can be maintained with the incident site and through which the resources of other agencies can be coordinated and mobilized. In an incident, each agency sets up a task force to pull together all its own resources of negotiators, psychiatrists, intelligence experts, and press spokesmen. This team is supplemented by representatives of other agencies as needed. But the lead agency has the basic responsibility of providing the core of the crisis management team. When problems which are not susceptible of decision at the level of operational crisis managers arise, the issues are referred to the National Security Council's Special Co-ordination Committee.

Insurgencies

Insurgencies arise whenever the constituents of a nation start developing incongruities with respect to the pillars of the unifying principle of nationalism, Arguably, viewed from one standpoint, it is a potent weapon, a sword of 'national' liberation and what they perceive as social justice; viewed from another, it is a subversive and sinister process exacerbating social dissension, causing political chaos and economic disruption. Patriotism, race, religion, the cry for social justice: beneath alt these symbolic and abstract causes that have inspired revolutions over the ages, there is a single driving principle. It is an upsurge of popular will, that really has not much to do with the questions of national or ethnic identity, self-determination, forms of government, or social justice, the familiar shibboleths of insurgency. In fact it is quite debatable whether relative economic deprivation in itself is the decisive factor that it is widely assumed to be, for it cannot be denied that poverty as well as oppression have been, after all, such conditions of life in the world that have been endured by countless generations without even a murmur. The 'will to revolt' is something more than a reaction to political circumstances or material conditions. It expresses a consciousness, not of 'causes' but of 'potentiality,' The effect of this consciousness is to produce a pervasive and urgent desire for radical change, that the conditions of life that had hitherto seemed immutable can, after all; be changed, Limitations that had been accepted without questions all at once become intolerable. The hint of imminent change suggests opportunities that had not been glimpsed until now. This gives birth to the will to 'act.' It makes for the realisation that here is something we can do, have, or be, simply by acting–then what have we been waiting for? Let us act! This describes the state of mind of the insurgent, whatever his slogans or his cause; and his ultimate weapon, above and beyond any questions of strategy, tactics or techniques of irregular warfare, is nothing more than the ability to inspire this state of mind in others. The defeat of the enemy in the military sense, the overthrow of the government and the installation of its own authority are secondary tasks in that they come later. The primary effort of the insurgent is to militate the population, and deprive the government of the consent of the people.

In this connection it should be pertinent to refer to two popular fallacies. They were quite prevalent among Western theorists for whom insurgency was, for quite some time, synonymous with communism. In the first fallacy they maintained that an insurgency is the deformed offspring of a process of artificial insemination, and that the insurgent nucleus is made up of outsiders, conspirators, political zombies–in other words, actual or spiritual aliens–who somehow stand separate from their social environment, while manipulating it to obscure and sinister ends. In the other fallacy they held that guerrilla warfare was essentially a matter of some special tactics and techniques, which could be adopted by just anyone who may have need of them, and that the adoption of these techniques was co-terminous with an insurgency. The first view is both naive and cynical. Reflecting the general, political condescension of the Western mind, it assumes that people in the mass are simpletons, too ignorant, unsophisticated and passive to think for themselves or to have either the will or the capacity to rise in rebellion. In the same spirit it further assumes that people would scarcely choose the revolutionary path of their own accord; and certainly not if the revolution in question was not in consonance with the political ideals held dear by the Americans. The second view obviously confuses a tool with the mechanic. Local military success will serve no purpose if the insurgency does not also weaken the morale of the government and its soldiers, strain the financial resources of the regime, and increase political pressure on it by creating widespread apprehension and dissatisfaction with the progress of a war in which there is no progress–and no end in sight. The intrinsic advantages of the insurgents make up for the intrinsic disadvantages of a government.

Modern governments are extremely vulnerable to insurgencies because they must, at all cost, keep the economy functioning and showing a profit or providing the materials and markets on which another, dominant economy depends. They are vulnerable because they must maintain the appearance of normalcy; they can be embarrassed out of office. And they are vulnerable because they cannot afford to be as ruthless as the situation demands. A government cannot afford to declare an all-out war against an insurgent situation. While the insurgent would love to wear down the government militarily, but his ultimate objective is to fan the fires of sedition, to raise as many people as possible against the regime, to discredit it, isolate it, wreck its credit, undermine its economy, over-extend its resources, and finally cause its disintegration. Insurgents who know their trade and have some popular support too cannot be eliminated by the means available to or even practicable by most governments. On the other hand, there are few governments which can stand the political, psychological, and economic stresses of insurgencies, no matter how strong they may be militarily. The dilemma of a modern government was very succinctly described by Theodore Sorenson, adviser to President J.F. Kennedy in the following words: "Our world-wide military primacy cannot produce a victory, and our world-wide political primacy cannot permit a withdrawal. We are unable to transfer our will to the South Vietnamese and unable to break the will of the North Vietnamese. Any serious escalation would risk Chinese or Soviet intervention, and any serious negotiations would risk a Communist South Vietnam." The insurgent derives his strength from his freedom from territorial commitments, his mobility, and his relationship to a discontented people, as the spokesman of their grievances,' the armed vanguard, as Che Guevara puts it, of militant social protest.

The Guerrilla Warfare

Some people are inclined to think that guerrilla warfare is a 20th century invention. While it is true that the post-World War II era has witnessed this style of warfare raised to its highest level, the fact is that guerrilla warfare has been practised by irregulars since the beginning of the history of armed conflict. Perhaps those practising guerrilla warfare in the past may not have known what they were doing, but the tactics, and frequently their strategies, were often the same as those used by guerrilla forces which succeeded in stalling the mightiest of armies. If there is anything new about guerrilla war, it is its use as a tool of political change.

To start with, the practitioner of irregular warfare must admit that due to his obvious inferiority in total power (that is, manpower plus firepower) he is not able to achieve a decisive victory through direct conventional combat.

If the Vietnam experiment has proved one thing, it is that the techniques and strategy of the guerrilla fighter, waging the war of the flea, have established their potency in the severest test imaginable short of a nuclear war, against the military might and technology of the world's richest and most powerful nation. It also provides that hardware is not the most important thing in war. Most people, journalists and politicians in particular, are prone to confuse technology with science. Hence they are not able to appreciate the fundamental truth that, irrespective of the impressive technological inventions, the principles of warfare remain essentially the same. Similarly, the problems of generalship also remain unaltered over the ages.

Hence, his first and foremost concern is that of self-preservation. He must minimise his losses–once who fights and runs away, lives to fight another day. This gave birth to the hackneyed phrase: 'hit and run' tactics. The purpose of the guerrilla is not to destroy the enemy by a few massive blows; his purpose is to continuously harass him–keep him under strain and wear him down. He should not expect quick results–he must learn to wait with infinite patience for the cumulative effect of those innumerous small engagements to tell upon the morale and resources of the opponent.

The guerrilla fighter has no option but to adopt dishonourable tactics in dealing with a strong adversary. He must refuse to give battle on the conditions of the enemy. He must appear elusive when the enemy is strong and resolute. He must engage the enemy only briefly and that too when it suits him, that is, he is able to strike with effect. By such repeated strikes he must wear the enemy down, by chipping away at the morale of the government troops and by inducing the maximum expenditure of funds, material, and manpower in the effort to suppress him. A successful guerrilla should not expect to be able to fight in isolation of the people–the population will hide him, and at the same time would reveal, from day to day and hour to hour, the disposition, strength and plans of the enemy. His strength must, on the other hand, lie in his dispersion and the extreme mobility of his lightly armed men without territorial or hardware investments and encumbrances. In the profound insight of Sun Tzu: "The enemy must not know where I intend to give battle. For if he does not know where I intend to give battle, he must prepare in a great many places. And when he prepares in a great many places, those I have to fight in anyone place will be few. ..And when he prepares everywhere, he will be weak everywhere."

Fortunes of an Insurgency

Insurgency is a complex and multifaceted phenomenon, having wide variations with respect to specific goals and strategies. In their quest for victory, insurgents have devised various strategies with a view to maximise the effectiveness of their overall political techniques and violence. These strategies can be differentiated by examining the relative importance they ascribe to six general variables: popular support, organisation, cohesion, external support, environment and effectiveness of the government.

For many theorists, popular support is an overriding strategic consideration: As Mao maintained: "The richest source of power to wage war lies in the masses of the people." The support of the people can be divided into two categories: active support and passive support. The active supporters are willing to risk personal sacrifice on behalf of the insurgents; the passive supporters merely sympathise with the aims and activities of the insurgents. The active supporters provide the insurgents with supplies, intelligence, shelter, concealment and, in some cases, even carry out protest activities. The number of passive supporters boosts the morale of the insurgents and relieves them of the fear of betrayal in a difficult situation.

It may so happen that the native population identifies itself spontaneously with the insurgents, making their task easier. However, if that does not happen, the insurgents must actively proselytise the people to convince them that their goals are both just and achievable. There are several methods of gaining the desired support. In some cases, assertive individuals emerge as the clearly identifiable leaders of insurgent movements. If they also happen to be blessed with theatrical and histrionic oratorical skills and forceful, dynamic personalities, they are frequently able to motivate others to join their cause by virtue of their example and persuasiveness. Mao,

Fidel Castro and Lenin belonged to this category. We shall describe the phenomenon as that of "charismatic attraction." A second means of obtaining popular support is an emphasis on "esoteric appeals." Directed mainly at the intellectuals, the esoteric appeals seek to clarify the situation by placing it in an ideological or theoretical context that orders and interprets political complexities. For example, the Marxist revolutionaries discovered that Lenin's exegesis on imperialism had an innate and powerful attraction in the Third World countries because it provided a coherent, logical, and all-encompassing explanation of the poverty, illiteracy and oppression that characterised their political and social milieu. Furthermore, by pointing a definitive finger at the indigenous feudal or capitalist classes and their links with external imperialist elements, it provides a readily identifiable target for the frustrations of the real and pseudo intellectuals. Even for the common people it helps greatly if the discontent is focused on a real villain. They are likely to welcome ideology if it brings about a clear identification of friend and foe. Moreover, it has been seen that doctrinal rationalisations for violence can themselves intensify discontent by increasing expectations and defending violence as a means to their attainment. On the other hand "exoteric appeals" focus on the concrete grievances of both the intelligentsia and the masses. These may involve problems like that of unemployment, corruption and repression by local officials, shortage of food, necessity of land reforms and other parameters of the physical quality of life like medical care, etc. The insurgents must hold out the promise that all these problems would be taken care of once they achieve their goal. It has also been pointed out that an ideology that appeals to national identity is the most powerful symbolic means of mobilising revolutionary support. The insurgents have only to merge powerfully enticing nationalist themes with esoteric and exoteric appeals. In order to impart some ideological credibility they have to manipulate some standard formulation such as Lenin's, and then blame the multinational corporations, neo-imperialism or liberalisation as the source of all national deprivations. This should provide an explanation, albeit simplified as well as a target for both the intellectuals and the masses. It may so happen that both esoteric and exoteric appeals do not work, may be because of government action and/or environmental disadvantages. Then they may turn to 'terrorism.' In this context, the purpose of terrorist acts is to obtain popular support by demonstrating the government's weaknesses in comparison to the strength of the insurgents. Trinquier points out that by making the people feel insecure it causes them to lose confidence in the government and to be drawn to the insurgents for protection. However, the targets need to be selected with great care.

An effective organisation is one the important ways of compensating for the material superiority of the opponents. When scholars maintain that insurgency is more a political phenomenon than a military one, they usually have in mind the great amount of effort the insurgents devote to organisation, either on the elite level, if it is a conspiracy, or the mass level, if it is an internal war-like situation. By virtue of an efficient organisation the insurgents are better able to perform two of their basic functions–provision of instrumental services and establishment of channels for expressive protest–that attract adherents. On the individual level, participation can yield material benefits, if the organisation has the resources, and it can generate a great deal of psychological satisfaction by virtue of the new sense of identity and self-worth that is produced by the perception that one is indeed engaged in a sublime common endeavour. For the insurgents to increase their following, they must increase the level of differentiation of the organisation (that is, its complexity). They must create parallel hierarchies to compete with the government institutions. The parallel hierarchy can take two forms: penetration of the existing official administrative structures by subversive agents, or creation of autonomous insurgent structures designed to take over full administrative responsibilities when the military-political conditions are deemed appropriate. The next step is to create functional auxiliaries such as youth groups, peasant organisations, workers' groups, women's organisations, etc. These auxiliaries are known as 'fronts' and they are considered invaluable in widening the support base of the movement. In addition to this differentiation of the political and the semi-political structures, the insurgents must diversify their military organisation too. This involved creation of logistics units, intelligence cells, terrorist networks, and full-time and part-time fighters, etc. The full-time fighters should operate from secure bases and focus on attacking government forces and installations.

The importance of unity within the ranks of the insurgents cannot be overemphasised. Given the fact that the insurgents have at their disposal a formidable arsenal of a all sorts of actions (ambushes, sabotage, kidnappings, assassinations, bombings, arson, etc.), they will be able to employ such diverse methods effectively only when they have a coordinated strategy. McCuen contends that unifying the effort is the basic principal behind all effective revolutionary strategy, planning, tactics and organisation.

Another important variable in deciding the fortune of an insurgency is the factor of environment. Among other things, this includes terrain, climate, road and communication, network, ethnicity, religion and culture size of the country, the state of its economic development and disparity among various regions, and the quantity and distribution of the people. There are a large number of examples from history to show that rugged terrain–vast mountains, jungles, swamps, forests and like–is eminently suited for successful guerrilla warfare. They provide inaccessible hideouts for the guerrillas, either for temporary purposes or for the so-called secure base and at the same time, hinder the movement of government forces. The vastness of the terrain is also important for the guerrilla. If the areas favourable for guerrilla operations are small, they can be easily isolated and penetrated. However, if the area is large, the insurgents can establish their pockets of influence at several places simultaneously, making it enormously difficult for the government administration and forces to deal with them all at once. In the first place the supervision of a large population will be difficult and secondly, it will generally not be possible for the government to commit an effective concentration of troops at all the places. In fact Mao regarded a vast countryside as a *sine qua non* of successful protracted war. Poor roads and communication favour the insurgents. If the road communication system is developed and extensive, government forces are at an advantage because they can move better and assert their technological superiority. Demographic factors also have an impact on an insurgency. For example, an urbanised environment discourages the formation of secure bases or liberated zones as the Government can easily monitor the activities of the citizens. Then societal cleavages on account of ethnicity, religion and language may also be exploited by the insurgents, particularly if the majority of the population is from the same ethnic, religious, and/or language groups as the insurgents, whereas the authorities are not. This is one of the important factors to be considered in Kashmir.

We shall discuss the importance of the role of the government at length when we discuss the counterinsurgency operations. Here it would suffice to note that the government's response is the pivotal variable in insurgencies, because where the government response is poor, the insurgents can tolerate shortcomings in popular and external support, organisation, cohesion and the environment. However, if the government response is characterised by a methodical approach and firm resolve, such shortcomings would spell disaster for the movement. In any case, where the government displays the ability and willingness to resist and the forces are not demoralised, the insurgents must be prepared for a prolonged conflict. Any hope of a quick victory must be ruled out in such cases. Then the insurgents must fall back on effectively organising the population, ensuring unity of effort, obtaining proper external support and exploiting whatever advantages the environmental factors have to offer.

The Maoist Approach to Insurgency

Mao presumes an enemy who is admittedly in a superior position, and then goes on to neutralise him by gaining strength from popular support, extensive organisational efforts and the environment as resources. He perceives a prolonged conflict before a consummate victory could be achieved. Mao prescribes a sequential approach to insurgency (or revolution) where each step is designed to take the insurgent closer to his goal and is dependent on the outcome of the step preceding it. In a way the Maoist approach can be regarded as the classical approach to insurgency; others can be treated as special cases or variants. We shall have a detailed discussion on the various steps involved in the Maoist approach when we discuss the various phases of insurgency.

The Maoist approach is a multifaceted one which emphasises several interrelated elements, namely, popular support, organisation and the environment. While it is possible for the insurgents to consciously control the first two factors, they must adapt themselves to their specific environmental conditions. The first task of the insurgent is to prepare the people for a prolonged conflict through a combination of propaganda efforts and organisational dexterity. Secondly, once the conflict ensues, they must sustain it and gradually expand their support to a point where they come to control the countryside, thereby isolating the urban centres. It should be obvious that the Maoist approach lends itself well to a situation where the insurgents, have a vast country to operate and which is on the lower side of the development spectrum in the sense of a poor roads and communication network. Mao does not regard external support highly and places great emphasis on self-reliance. However, we do not think that modern practitioners of the Maoist approach would mind external support, especially in offsetting a similar assistance to the government side. The Maoist approach has its vulnerabilities too, as the entire exercise demands flexibility and coordinated efforts on the part of many insurgents, who may be exposed to the government's psychological, organisational and military countermeasures. Much, therefore, depends on their political and military skins and emotional commitment to the cause.

Many people tend to simplify guerrilla war as a war of attrition. This is not a very accurate description. The guerrilla war prescribed by Mao is not so much abrasive as it is subversive. It is a growth that penetrates the crevices of a rotting structure and is eventually capable of bursting it as under. It is often wondered as to how could an ill-equipped guerrilla group that does not have the backing of an industrial system defeat one that has the necessary material support. Katzenbach argues that Mao's approach was simply to shift the emphasis customarily given to the fundamental components of previous military doctrines. Where the industrial nations stressed such tangible military factors as arms, logistics and manpower, Mao emphasised the intangibles: time, space and will. Admitting the inferiority in arms and firepower with which to confront a regular well-equipped army in the field, Mao decided that it was best to avoid battle by surrendering territory. By doing so, he managed to trade space for time, and used the time to produce will, that is, the psychological capacity of the people to resist defeat. His fundamental belief is that only those who will admit defeat can be defeated. Mao's military problem was how to organise space so that it could be made to yield time for his celebrated 'protracted war.' His political problem was how to organise time so that it could be made to yield will, the quality which makes willingness to sacrifice the order of the day. Western military theorists tend to get obsessed with the idea of finishing a war; Mao's overriding concern was to keep it going. The true guerrilla must avoid a military decision until he is in a position to dictate his terms. The answer lay in giving way before a determined advance of the enemy, and, like the sea, close in again as the enemy passes. Time is required, not only for political mobilisation, but also to allow the inherent weaknesses of the enemy to develop and get magnified under the stress of war. The insurgents must wait for going on to the offensive till their total strength has reached a level comparable to that of the enemy–then it should not be the hit and run tactics but open battles.

The Purpose of Terrorism

The purpose of terrorism is selective intimidation of recalcitrant individuals or groups. But this cannot be carried too far. An excess is bound to lead to adverse reaction from the people. They could even be driven into supporting the government if the administration could offer them security. However, when directed prudently against selected targets perceived as supporters of the regime or considered vital for it otherwise, the efficacy of terrorism is never in doubt. As Crozier described it: "A common purpose is to make life unendurable for the enemy." Terrorising the key institutions of the government and thus bringing about a paralysis in the functioning of the administration has manifold results. If the police is the target, terror causes a sort of disillusionment set in, leading the force to a state of shock and inactivity. Conversely if the government persists in trying to stamp out terrorism under the pressure of the people and the media, the resources of the police and the army are greatly stretched, making them even less effective. Moreover, there is a clamouring from a large section of the people, the media and even the ruling group for what they perceive as a panacea in the days of participative democracies, that is, a dialogue, which is essentially nothing but a tacit admission that the regime has buckled up and is prepared to grant some concessions. As the Governor General of Algeria Jacques Soustelle described it: "Terror is a psychological weapon of unbelievable power. Before the bodies of those whose throats have been cut and the grimacing faces of the mutilated, all capacity for resistance lapses; the spring is broken." Terrorism is thus found to be a particularly potent tool against regimes which lack resolve, which are weak-kneed, and which lack the moral courage to face some the harsh realities built in their socio-political system. As we have had occasion to witness time and again, down from the release of terrorists following certain kidnappings in the early days of insurgency in Kashmir to the release of foreign mercenaries following the hijacking of IC-814, the soft state of India is particularly prone to this sort of backmail. Since unlike most of the countries of Europe and even some of Asia which have gone through a horrific amount of human suffering and bloodshed in the wars of the twentieth century, this country has not had a real baptism through blood, the Indian society has developed a morbid fear of violence. This has made the Indian society highly vulnerable to acts of terrorism–intelligent terrorists can certainly extort more out of the Indian state than they can ever expect from a principled and resolute state.

Final Stage of Insurgency

The final stage of a classical insurgency is the mobile or conventional warfare stage. It is presumed that by this time the insurgents must have established a 'government' in one of their 'liberated zones' or a 'government-in-exile' in one of the neighbouring countries friendly to their cause. Although it would be nothing more than a front to the revolutionary political network, it appears democratic to appeal to the population. Furthermore, by arguing it to be representing the 'aspirations of the people' it can be used at various international fora to mobilise the world opinion in favour of the insurgents. Militarily, this is the phase of the 'strategic offensive' for the insurgents when their own force level has become comparable to that of the government. The objective at this point is the displacement of the regime through military defeats inflicted upon it. The guerrilla units should have, by now, switched over to the pattern of conventional forces as mobile columns up to divisional strength, capable of engaging and defeating government forces in open, pitched battles. It should be obvious that for this stage the logistics requirements of the insurgents would increase greatly. Although the die-hard communist romanticists would not love it, practical wisdom demands that external support, at least in terms of logistic requirements, must be necessarily obtained at this stage. The small guerrilla bands would then play only an ancillary role. In this connection, Mao placed great emphasis on achieving numerical superiority.

In this stage the government finds itself faced with the second dilemma of counterinsurgency warfare. General Vo Nguyen Giap described it in the following graphic words: "Either they try to extend their strong-points once again, with their depleted manpower, in which case, they must spread themselves thin, and lay themselves open to new attacks that we can launch in regimental or divisional strength, or else they try to reduce these strong-points and consolidate them, which frees territory and population to us. Our guerrillas and government take over within gunshot of their strong-points. In most cases, we are actually besieging them. The minute a soldier pops out of a blockhouse, he faces guerrilla fire." In other words, the more the government holds, the more they have to defend and the broader is the insurgent target area. Yet on the other hand, the more the insurgent fights and wins, the more he has with which to fight and to win. The government would seek to end the war as quickly as possible, in order to minimise its losses; the insurgent would seek to prolong it, since he has everything to gain by it.

It should however, be noted that even in this stage the insurgents do not expect a quick victory. The revolutionary theory admits and provides for the defeats which could possibly be inflicted upon the insurgents who have but recently started fighting as regulars. Mao prescribed that after a severe defeat the insurgents must fall back to a preceding phase–perhaps from mobile to guerrilla warfare or guerrilla warfare to terrorism–until the rebel forces can rebuild and try again. General Giap had switched back to guerrilla warfare from mobile warfare after he suffered reverses at the hands of Marshal de Lattre de Tassigny in 1951. Thus the government will be faced with the task of not only defeating the insurgents, but keep on defeating them as they fall back from phase to phase. Unfortunately, most governments fail to follow this path because they are not able to adjust their strategy to correspond with the changes in the insurgent operations.

The ultimate aim of the insurgents in the mobile warfare stage is to make the countryside untenable for the government, then seizing the villages and the larger towns, driving the army back into its urban strongholds, which once isolated, can be reduced piecemeal. As a French officer described their final situation in Indochina's Red River Delta, the government forces would find themselves engulfed like *'des grumeaux dans la soupe'* (breadcrumbs in the soup). The classical theory of insurgency maintain that finally the government forces would withdraw or surrender piecemeal.

Real insurgencies in the modern world need not necessarily follow the successive stages of a classical insurgency. Every country has got its unique features and problems. The interplay of all such factors may result in the insurgency acquiring a unique character of its own. People react differently in different countries. In the Indian context, a study of the Indian psyche reveals that it should be nearly impossible to subvert a significant number of people by any ideology, and least of all by any communist oriented ideology. Relatively more potent factors are to be found among race, religion and what could be perceived as political injustice. Since the Indians, by their very nature, show a pronounced lack of enthusiasm for commitment to an ideology of the revolutionary kind, it can be safely argued that the organisational aspects of any insurgency in the country will be considerably weak. If an insurgent situation in the country makes a claim for popular support, the reasons for it should be sought elsewhere. For example, in Kashmir it was a combination of identity crisis based on race and religion, and a history of perceived political injustice. These factors were abetted by the latent opportunism of some people who nursed hopes of a quick capitulation on the part of the Indian government. Although there are sufficient indicators of the fact that there was subversion and that those people did sympathise with the insurgents, the conspiratorial network could really never penetrate the society to such an extent as to become an integral part of it. The subversion of the people and their support were strictly opportunistic in character.

As we have stated elsewhere, the Indian society and political system are particularly vulnerable to the terrorism aspect of insurgency. That is how most insurgencies in the country tend to regress to the terrorism stage. However, the response of the administration in several cases is so poor, ill-conceived and misdirected that it permits the simultaneous existence of more than one phase. Thus we find situations where very distinct aspects of the guerrilla warfare stage are coexisting with the terrorism stage. There are any, number of attacks by the insurgents which can only be classified under the guerrilla warfare stage. Yet that does not happen to be their mainstay and they keep on taking recourse to terrorism. We are, therefore, forced to conclude that if an insurgency in the country shows signs of progression up to the guerrilla warfare stage, it is not so much on account of the intrinsic merits of the movement as on account of the hopeless response of the administration. In any case, the insurgents also seem to have realised that their strength and the Indian government's weakness lies in terrorism. Since the security forces of the country are notable to do better, the borders of the country are essentially porous. Thus the insurgents depend greatly on external support in the sense that almost all of their requirements of weapons, shelter, training, etc., are met extremely conveniently from across the border. Unlike the classical insurgents they do not have to bother at all with acquiring popular support, establishing bases and collecting weapons by looting from the government forces. Moreover, committing acts of terrorism with the help of modern technology is so easy and free of risk that most insurgents are tempted into relying on it all too often.

We maintain that the Indian society and political system have inherent cracks that would get magnified under the stress of a determined and sustained phase of terrorism. The weakest links in the system are the people and the media. Before anybody else cracks up, the people and the media would crack up. Public opinion in this country is determined largely by the trash which is fed to the public by the print and electronic media. Since they are the most irresponsible and intellectually most bankrupt lot, they would take the lead in softening the resolve of the people. Let us not forget that it is the same media which has not only failed in condemning our acts of capitulation before terrorism, but has gone to the extent of suggesting that for the sake of peace we could pardon all the insurgents who have killed thousands of people! It is the same media which exulted in eulogising insurgents like Abdul Majid Dar the moment he showed the slightest inclination of talking with the government. It is the same media which started referring to the Hizb-ul-Mujahideen insurgents as 'Hizb-ul-Mujahideen commanders' when they came for talks and accorded them a respect which would have been due only to representatives of a sovereign nation at war with us. We maintain that the pseudo-intellectuals of the country (who have excellent relations with the media) and its media are capable of reacting to a sustained phase of terrorism in such an effeminate manner that their wailing would build up an unbearable pressure on the leaders who too would have no dearth of people with essentially the same bent of mind and character, predisposing them to react in a very predictable manner. We suggest that no responsible citizen should ever forget the most shameful manner in which we had capitulated before the hijackers of flight IC-814. It contained the seeds of some very bad omens. We strongly maintain that professional insurgents have only to maintain a certain level of terrorist violence to make the people, the media and the leaders sick of it. After that the developments would take care of themselves. For example, foreign investors would lose no time in running away the moment their interests start getting systematically targeted. Then at isolated places there may be such police or army excesses as to lead to mass protests. In short, if the insurgents are able to use terrorist violence in such a manner as to act as a catalyst for the innate disruptive tendencies in the country, an uncontrollable and unpredictable chain reaction may result which will bring us perilously close to a climate of collapse.

The insurgents are very much aware of the possibilities of an insurgency sustained by external support escalating into a full-fledged war, or the unwelcome intervention of the international community. As scholars of insurgencies and counterinsurgency operations, let us also keep in mind that in this age of consumerism indoctrination is *passe.* If there is still somebody who dreams of a revolution, he must be a fool. However, that should not lull us into complacence. The objective of the foregoing discourse is to make us aware of our own weaknesses and vulnerabilities, and the dangers we are faced with on account of them. The objective is to prepare us mentally for coping with precisely such situation. Forewarned is four-armed. Only when we realise that we have a predilection for reacting in a certain manner, would we be able to make conscious efforts to override the tendency. Let us not be afraid mythical insurgency that could, on its own, lead to a secession from India. Let us be afraid of ourselves lest we are bullied or terrorised into ceding to some unjust demands, which would bring eternal disgrace to this great nation of ours.

The killing of policemen serves to demoralise the police; the killing of civilians raises the general level of violence in the area, thereby increasing the pressure on the government for the deteriorating law and order situation. Thus a single act serves more than one minor purpose and ultimately the single larger purpose of the insurgency. The insurgent does not stand to gain anything particularly special or beneficial by specifically targeting the armed forces only–it is for him to select his targets, and he is under no delusion that by selecting military targets his moral stature would be increased. Perhaps the aforementioned theorists did not realise that acts of terrorism (like murder, torture, mutilation, bombing, kidnapping, etc.) could be committed on military targets with equal facility and effect. Perhaps they are not aware that in Kashmir the insurgents have gone to the extent of kidnapping solitary soldiers of the BSF who had gone outside their bunkers to answer the call of nature–these soldiers were killed after horrible torture. Or perhaps they have not heard that once in an ambush in Kashmir when the armymen ran out of ammunition, they were killed after elaborate torture and mutilation of their bodies. Perhaps they have forgotten that even in Cyprus a constable of the Special Branch was shot dead before a crowd of hundreds (August 28, 1955) by a young government clerk, Michael Karaolis, a member of a three-man EOKA execution squad. Thus we conclude that the distinction between terrorism and guerrilla warfare is of any meaning or consequence only when they are discussed in the context of a definite progression of insurgency, and that too for largely a theoretical purpose. They ought not to be treated as qualitatively different tools. For the purpose of the theoretical study we are going to undertake, the more important underlying principle is that of coercive intimidation. Whether the insurgent kills a civilian or a soldier, his concern is not so much with the immediate target as with the wider target group, that is, the government, which is intended to be coerced into accepting the ultimate demands of the insurgents under the pressure of the climate of fear generated by the killing. And it should not be lost sight of that even in a classical insurgency, the effect of guerrilla warfare is accorded as much importance for its psychological aspect of chipping away the morale of the forces (and thus the government) as for its purely military aspect of causing attrition. Losses in hardware can be easily compensated by large nation states; losses in morale cannot be. It was quite common in Central America for terrorism to be used in conjunction with rural guerrilla and economic and political warfare in about bids to topple governments. Thus the treatment of terrorism in isolation must be regarded as an aberration found with some theorists of Western Europe and North America only.

3

International Terrorism

Hijackings

The advent of what is considered modern, international terrorism occurred on 22 July 1968. On that day three armed Palestinian terrorists, belonging to the Popular Front for the Liberation of Palestine (PFLP), one of the six groups then comprising the Palestine Liberation Organization (PLO), hijacked an Israeli EIAI commercial flight *en route* from Rome to Tel Aviv. Although commercial aircraft had been hijacked before (this was the twelfth such incident in 1968 alone), the EIAI hijacking differed significantly from all previous ones. First, its purpose was not simply the diversion of a scheduled flight from one destination to another, such as had been happening since 1959 with a seemingly endless succession of homesick Cubans or sympathetic revolutionaries from other countries commandeering domestic American passenger aircraft simply as a means to travel to Cuba. This hijacking was a bold political statement. The terrorists who seized the EIAI flight had done so with the express purpose of trading the passengers they held hostage for Palestinian terrorists imprisoned in Israel. Second, unlike previous hijackings, where the origin or nationality of the aircraft that was being seized did not matter (as long as the plane itself was capable of transporting the hijacker(s) to a desired destination), EIAI–as Israel's national airline and by extension, therefore, a readily evident national 'symbol' of the Israeli state–had been specifically and deliberately targeted by the terrorists. Third, by engineering a crisis where the consequences of a government ignoring or rejecting the terrorists' demands could prove catastrophic, leading to the destruction of the aircraft and the deaths of all persons on board, the terrorists succeeded in forcing their avowed enemy, Israel, to communicate directly with them and therefore with the organization to which they belonged, despite the Israeli Governments previous declarations and policy pronouncements to the contrary. Finally, through the combination of dramatic political statement, 'symbolic' targeting and crisis-induced *de facto* recognition, the terrorists discovered that they had the power to create major media events–especially when innocent civilians were involved. As Zehdi Labib Terzi, the PLO's chief observer at the United Nations, reflected in a 1976 interview, "The first several hijackings aroused the consciousness of the world and awakened the media–and world opinion much more and more effectively–than 20 years of pleading at the United Nations."

Many of the post-war anti-colonial terrorist campaigns, as noted above, also had a prominent international orientation. However, with the EIAI hijacking the nature and character of terrorism demonstrably changed. For the first time, terrorists began to travel regularly from one country to another to carry out attacks. In addition, they also began to target innocent civilians from other countries who often had little if anything to do with the terrorists cause or grievance, simply in order to endow their acts with the power to attract attention and publicity that attacks against their declared or avowed enemies often lacked. Their intent was to shock and, by shocking, to stimulate worldwide fear and alarm.

These dramatic tactical changes in terrorism were facilitated by the technological advances of the time that had transformed the speed and ease of international commercial air travel and vastly improved both the quality of television news footage and the promptness with which that footage could be broadcast around the globe. Accordingly, terrorists rapidly came to appreciate that operations perpetrated in countries other than their own and directly involving or affecting foreign nationals were a reliable means of attracting attention to themselves and their cause.

At the forefront of this transformation were the constituent groups of the PLO. Between 1968 and 1980, Palestinian terrorist groups were indisputably the world's most active, accounting for more *international* terrorist incidents than any other movement. The success achieved by the PLO in publicizing the Palestinians' plight through the 'internationalization' of its struggle with Israel has since served as a model for similarly aggrieved ethnic and nationalist minority groups everywhere, demonstrating how long-standing but hitherto ignored or forgotten causes can be resurrected and dramatically thrust on to the world's agenda through a series of well-orchestrated, attention-grabbing acts. In order to understand how revolutionary a development this was, it is necessary briefly to review the Palestinians' recent history and to appreciate the depths of obscurity and international neglect from which the PLO emerged.

Palestinian Terrorist Activities

Yet although Palestinian terrorist activities precipitated a significant international crisis (Suez) and eleven years later led to a major regional war–and notwithstanding the plight of hundreds of thousands of Palestinian refugees, man of whom were still living in the abject poverty of squalid refugee camps nearly two decades after their exile had begun–few outside the region took any notice of, much less cared about, the Palestinians. In fact, it was not until after 1968, when the *fedayeen* took their struggle against Israel outside the Middle East and began deliberately to enmesh citizens from more distant countries in their struggle, that the Palestinians discovered an effective means of broadcasting their cause to the world and attracting its attention and sympathy. "When we hijack a plane it has more effect than if we killed a hundred Israelis in battle," the PF1P's founder and leader Dr. George Habash explained in a 1970 interview–echoing the same point made a decade earlier by the F1N's Ramdane Abane. "For decades world opinion has been neither for nor against the Palestinians," Habash noted. "It simply ignored us. At least the world is talking about us now."

The premier example of terrorism's rower to rocket a cause from obscurity to renown, however, was without doubt the murder of eleven Israeli athletes seized by Palestinian terrorists at the 1972 Munich Olympic Games. The purpose of the operation, according to Fuad al-Sharnali, one of its architects, was to capture the world's attention by striking at a target of inestimable value (a country's star athletes), in a setting calculated to provide the terrorists with unparalleled exposure and publicity (the top global sporting event). "Bombing attacks on ElAI offices do not serve our cause," al-Shamali had argued." "We have to kill their most important and most famous people. Since we cannot come close to their statesmen, we have to kill artists and sportsmen."

The incident began on 5 September 1972, shortly before 5.00 a.m., when eight terrorists belonging to the PLO's Black September Organization (BSO) burst into the Israelis' dormitory, killing two athletes immediately and taking nine other hostage. As news of the attack spread and police rushed to the scene, the site was cordoned off and the terrorists issued their demands. They offered to exchange the hostages for 236 Palestinians imprisoned in Israeli gaols and five other terrorists being held in Germany (including Andreas Baader and Ulrike Meinhof, the founders of the radical left-wing West German terrorist group, the Red Army Faction); and they wanted a guarantee of safe passage to any Arab country (except Lebanon or Jordan). They also threatened to begin killing one hostage every two hours if their demands were not met. Fifteen hours of negotiations followed until a deal, brokered by the West Germans, was struck. The terrorists and their hostages, it was agreed, would be transported in two helicopters to the airbase at Furstenfeldbruck, where they would then board a Lufthansa 727 aircraft and depart for Cairo. Once in Egypt, the exchange of prisoners would be effected and the terrorists allowed to proceed whenever they wished. The Egyptians, however, later changed their mind and decided to refuse the aircraft landing rights.

At 10.35 p.m. the two helicopters touched down at the German air base. Two terrorists emerged and went to inspect the airliner parked nearby. Two others took up positions outside the helicopters. The remaining four terrorists stayed inside, guarding the nine Israelis. Suddenly shots rang out. As part of a pre-arranged rescue plan, five West German police sharpshooters had opened fire. Three of the four terrorists outside the helicopters were cut down: the survivor, Mohammad Masalhah, the group's commander, took cover.

The other terrorists immediately began to return fire and, according to some accounts, started to kill the hostages. A tense stand-off now ensued as appeals were broadcast over loudspeakers in Arabic, German and English to the remaining five terrorists to release their hostages and surrender. The terrorists again responded with gunfire. Finally, just after midnight, as German police prepared to mount a rescue assault, a terrorist leaped from one of the helicopters and tossed a hand grenade back into the cabin behind him. Pandemonium broke out when the grenade exploded. In the fire fight that erupted, two more terrorists, including Masalhah, were killed. The three remaining terrorists, however, kept police at bay until nearly 1.30 a.m., when they finally surrendered and were taken into custody. All nine hostages lay dead, along with a West German policeman.

Both operations-the hostage seizure and the rescue attempt–were colossal failures. The Palestinians had not only failed to obtain their principal, stated demand–the release of terrorists imprisoned in Israel and West Germany–but, to many observers, had irredeemably tarnished the righteousness of their cause in the eyes of the world. Indeed, international opinion was virtually unanimous in its condemnation of the terrorists' operation. The grisly denouement on the airfield tarmac, broadcast via television and radio throughout the world, was initially regarded as disastrous to the Palestinian cause: a stunning failure and a grave miscalculation, generating revulsion rather than sympathy and condemnation instead of support.

As for the failure to save the hostages, for many other countries as well as for West Germany the botched rescue attempt provided stark evidence of both how serious a threat international terrorism had become and how woefully inadequate their own counter-terrorist capabilities were. The embarrassed West Germans lost little time in establishing a special anti-terrorist detachment of their border police, known as GSG-9 (Grenzschutzgruppe Neun). Five years later, it acquitted itself brilliantly in Mogadishu, Somalia, rescuing all eighty-six hostages on board a Lufthansa flight hijacked *en route* from Mallorca by a mixed team of Palestinian and West German terrorists. In this incident, in marked contrast to the debacle at Furstenfeldbruck, the GSG-9 commandos killed three of the hijackers and captured the fourth before they could harm any of the hostages (one GSG-9 officer was wounded in the rescue assault as well as four hostages). In France, the Groupe d'Intervention de la Gendarmerie Nationale (GIGN) was created within the Gendarmerie Nationale as that country's dedicated counter-terrorist unit, in Britain, the elite Special Air Services Regiment (SAS) was given permission to establish a Counter-Revolutionary Warfare detachment with a specific counter-terrorism mission.

In 1980, these SAS units successfully resolved the six-day siege at the Iranian embassy in Princes Gate, London, rescuing nineteen of the twenty-one hostages (two died during the rescue operation) and killing five of the six terrorists. Curiously, at the time the United States decided *not* to follow the example of its European, allies and established no special, elite counter-terrorist unit of its own–thus courting the disaster that came to light years later in the failed attempt to rescue the fifty-two Americans held hostage at the US Embassy in Tehran. Instead, President Richard Nixon ordered the formation of a special Inter-Departmental Working Group on Terrorism (chaired by the then Secretary of State, Henry Kissinger) and elected to concentrate on diplomatic initiatives in the UN and elsewhere, focusing on the adoption of international conventions against terrorism.

The real lesson of Munich, however, was a somewhat counterintuitive one. The Olympic tragedy provided the first clear evidence that even terrorist attacks which fail to achieve their ostensible objectives can nonetheless still be counted successful provided that the operation is sufficiently dramatic to capture the media's attention. In terms of the publicity and exposure accorded to the Palestinian cause, Munich was an unequivocal success–a point conceded by even the most senior PLO officials. According to Abu Iyad, the organization's intelligence chief, long-time confidant of Arafat and co-founder with him of al-Fatah, the Black September terrorists admittedly "didn't bring about the liberation of any of their comrades imprisoned in Israel as they had hoped, but they did attain the operation's other two objectives: World opinion was forced to take note of the Palestinian drama, and the Palestinian people imposed their presence on an international gathering that had sought to exclude them."

The Armenians, had waged an inchoate armed struggle against Ottoman rule during the 1880s and 1890s in hopes of eliciting

Western sympathy and intervention. Their revolt had culminated in 1896 with the daring but ill-fated seizure of the Ottoman Bank in Constantinople. This event was followed by three days of intense anti-Armenian rioting and bloodshed during which untold numbers of Armenians lost their lives. Thereafter, most overt manifestations of Armenian nationalism lapsed into temporary abeyance; and those that did surface were forcibly suppressed. Nationalist activity was rekindled, however, during the First World War, mostly as a result of Russian efforts to foment Armenian unrest and thereby undermine the common enemy, Turkey. Ottoman suspicions of their Armenian subjects' loyalty, already aggravated by these Russian interventions, were further inflamed by the Armenians' refusal to support the Turkish war effort. Accordingly in 1915, Taalat Pasha, the Ottoman Interior Minister, ordered the Armenians' expulsion from their traditional homelands in eastern Turkey to Syria and Iraq. Although the exact number of Armenians who perished at this time of widespread war and upheaval remains a matter of considerable debate, the figure most commonly cited is 1.5 million people–roughly 60 per cent of Turkey's Armenian population. The events of 1915, therefore, are often cited as the first state 'genocide' of the twentieth century.

By the early 1980s, the Armenians' use of terrorism had apparently paid off. "Thus it is true that the re-emergence of the Armenian question in the news and especially of the Armenian genocide–is largely owing to Armenian terrorists," wrote Gerard Chaliand, a French Armenian scholar and one of the world's foremost authorities on terrorism and guerrilla warfare, in 1983. A year earlier, in a study of the Armenian terrorist movements, Andrew Corsun, one of the US State Department's leading analysts of terrorism, similarly argued that "by resorting to terrorism, Armenian extremists were able to accomplish in 5 years what legitimate Armenian organizations have been trying to do for almost 70 years internationalize the Armenian cause." However, while publicity and exposure proved to be easily gained through terrorism, the Armenian groups also found that attention does not necessarily translate into more tangible gains. For example, a detailed empirical study of American network news coverage of Armenian terrorism between 1968 and 1983 concluded that while the terrorist campaign had certainly increased public name recognition of the Armenians, it had not engendered any "meaningful awareness or sensitivity about the Armenians' cause, (their historical condition, or their political aims. More critical, perhaps, was the fact that, unlike the Palestinians, the vast-majority of the world wide Armenian diaspora did not rally to, much less actively support, the terrorists. Despite expressions of understanding of the terrorists' goals and motivations, the Armenian community offered them little overt assistance and became increasingly alienated by the violent acts committed in its name. What minimal actual support did exist began to dry up following the 1983 Orly Airport attack, to the point where, by the end of the decade, none of the Armenian terrorist groups was still actively engaged in international terrorism.

Internationalization of Terrorism

The 'internationalization' of terrorism that occurred in the late 1960s and early 1970s was not solely a product of Palestinian influence and success. Outside the Middle East, a combination of societal malaise and youthful idealism, rebelliousness and anti-militarism/anti-imperialism was rapidly transforming the collective political consciousness among the more affluent countries of Western Europe and North America. Perhaps the unprecedented economic prosperity of these years allowed the luxury of introspection and self-criticism that, in more radical political circles, generated a revulsion against the socio-economic inequities endemic to the modern, industrialized capitalist state. "All they can think about," Ulrike Meinhof the political activist and radical newspaper columnist turned Red Army Faction (RAF) terrorist, once dismissively remarked of her follow Germans, "is some hairspray; a vacation in Spain, and a tiled bathroom."

The sharp contrast between the highest and the lowest domestic levels of wealth and consumer consumption was further accentuated by the growing economic disparity between the developed world and the undeveloped world–as it came to be called, the 'Third World.' This was attributed by radicals as much to the 'neo-colonialist' ethos and economic exploitation inherent in capitalism as to the interventionist foreign policy championed by the United States under the banner of fighting the spread of communism. Thus by the late 1960s, opposition to America's involvement in Indochina had emerged as the principal rallying cry for politically engaged, disaffected youth everywhere. "Anti-imperialism meant first of all the protest against the Vietnam War, but also (against) the American predominance over most countries of the Third World," the former RAF terrorist Christoph Wackerngel explained in a recent speech recounting his own experience.

Indeed, to a great extent, the Red Army Faction (German: Rote Armee Fraktion; more popularly known as the Baader-Meinhof Group) and its sister terrorist organization, the Second of June Movement, encapsulated the revolutionary spirit and anti-establishment attitudes typical of left-wing terrorists in other Western countries at the time. Both groups emerged from the communes and student associations that were part of the 'counterculture' in late-1960s West Germany, and it was consequently impossible to separate their radical politics from their 'alternative' lifestyles. Revolution and armed struggle went hand-in-hand with sexual promiscuity and drug use. "You must understand," Astrid Proll, a member of the RAF's 'first generation,' later explained, "that then the most fantastic thing in the world was not to be a rock star, but a revolutionary."

With the end of the Vietnam War, the German terrorist in both the RAF and other groups needed to find a new cause. Their choice again reflected the international orientation of West Geman radical politics: common cause was not to be made with the Palestinians. In his book, Baumann described the logic behind this decision. "Since Vietnam is finished," the argument ran, "people should get involved with Palestine. It is actually much closer to us, which is apparent today with the oil business, and has more to do with us here in the European cities than does Vietnam. This was to become the new framework to carry on the struggle here."

The Palestinians were in fact the obvious candidates. As far back as 1968 the PLO–and Habash's PFLP especially–had welcomed terrorists from around the world to their guerrilla camps in Jordan for training, indoctrination and the general building of transnational revolutionary bridges. In this respect, the Palestinians pioneered the 'networking' dimension of international terrorism still in evidence among many groups today. In 1969 the Palestinians had welcomed the first delegation of West German terrorist–Baumann's comrades in the 'Bules' group, an early precursor of the Second of June Movement–to their guerrilla training camps in Jordan: "They got some training there; how to shoot; how to make bombs; how to fight," Baumann recalled. "But the Palestinians told them to go back to Germany and make propaganda for them. That was all they were hot for–they offered no weapons. The following year another party of German terrorists–including Andreas Baader, 'Gudrun Ensslin, Ulrike Meinhof and six of their colleagues–secretly made their way to Beirut and thence to Palestinian terrorist camps in Jordan, as much to escape the police dragnet closing in on them at home as to receive training as 'urban guerrillas.' Although relations between the Germans and their Palestinian hosts were strained to the point where, after two months, the group was asked to leave, Baader and company had by this time learned enough to enable them formally to establish their own terrorist group–the RAF. According to Rapoport, this development marked a significant milestone in the history of terrorism, since it was probably the first time that one terrorist group had trained another.

The Germans also reportedly provided critical logistical assistance to the Palestinian Black September terrorists responsible for the Munich massacre. Although the closest ties were forged with PFLP, Arafat's comparatively more moderate al-Fatah organization played a particularly important role in supplying the RAF with weapons. Its political agents in Germany, assigned primarily to fund-raising activities, operated a profitable business on the side selling hand-guns to the RAF. Indeed, according to the leading German-Israeli counter-terrorism analyst Dr. David Schiller, without the assistance provided by the Palestinian terrorists to their German counterparts the latter could not have survived.

The profound influence exercised by the Palestinians over the Germans was perhaps never clearer than in 1985, when the RAF joined forces with the French left-wing terrorist organization, Direct Action (in French, *Actioll Directe*, thus AD), in hopes of creating a PLO-like umbrella 'anti-imperialist front of Western European guerrillas' that could include Italy's Red Brigades (RB) and the Belgian Communist Combatant Cells (CCC) as well. But, just as the Armenians' and South Moluccans' attempts to replicate the PLO's success had foundered, so did the efforts of German and French organizations. Within two years, the promised campaign of 'Euroterrorism' against NATO's politico-military structure had fizzled out. The global conditions that had produced and nurtured these organizations, indeed, had endowed them with their fundamental *raison d'etre*, were changing more rapidly than they could adapt, thus threatening to turn them into hopeless anachronisms. Crippled by the arrests of the leading members of the French and Belgian groups, the 'anti-imperialist front' fell into disarray. Not surprisingly, perhaps, the Red Brigades shortly afterwards drifted into complete lassitude. The forty-year revolutionary struggle they had once so proudly proclaimed for the Italian people less than a decade earlier had run out of stream before even a generation had passed. In Germany, meanwhile, the RAF disconsolately carried on, despite the political revolutions then transforming the Soviet Union and Eastern Europe. The fall of the Berlin Wall in 1989 and the national reunification that followed deprived the group of their ideological resilience as well as a convenient cross-border sanctuary. Politically marginalized and bereft of either patron or safe haven, the RAF finally collapsed in 1992 under the weight of its own exhaustion and the indifference of those in the newly united Germany whom the group still purporated to represent.

4

The Kashmir Problem

Introduction

Kashmir must demand the utmost attention of all the concerned citizens for a host of reasons. In the first place we have the problem of insurgency *per se*. The state has been beset with violence since 1988. Indeed there were times when the sentiments of the average Kashmiri were so strongly aroused that the state was witnessing a full blown insurgency. It is only recently that the situation has improved somewhat in the sense of having progressed from the ambience of an insurgency to terrorism. Then it should also be kept in mind that Kashmir is a Muslim majority border state where Pakistan has a much deeper and more direct involvement than at any other place. Thirdly, the state has suffered miserably in the course of the violence. Since 1988, the state has witnessed the gruesome killing of at least 8,252 civilians in ten years. In the same period 9,098 alleged terrorists were also killed by the security forces at the cost of 1,768 casualties among their own ranks. Insurgency has reached such a level in Kashmir that in spite of all these killings of terrorists there are still about 3,500–4,000 active terrorists in the state with AK rifles, RPD/PK machineguns, rocket propelled grenade launchers, mortars, 107 mm rockets and a variety of explosive devices. To control these insurgents, we have been obliged to turn Kashmir into one of the most heavily militarised zones in the entire world. For internal security duty alone, that is, leaving aside the regular deployment on the border/LOC, we have three full corps of the army, besides a large number of battalions of the so called Rashtriya Rifles. Then there are about 600 companies of the various paramilitary forces including the BSF, the CRPF and the ITBP. It is a different thing that even all these men have not been able to make a material difference in the situation. A situation is certainly not normal, or anywhere near it, if we are obliged to retain our hold with the help of so many arms. In fact if somebody insists on harping on the use of the word 'normal' for his own political ends, the readers are reminded that it should be a perfect case of SNAFU, that is, 'situation normal, all fucked up'! The severity of the problem in Kashmir can be judged from a single fact, which does not lend itself to any distortion, that over 20,000 AK rifles have so far been recovered from the terrorists! More than 1,000 machine guns and RPG launchers each have been recovered! The number of the rounds of ammunition recovered is in excess of 32 lakhs! We are dealing with the matter in an objective manner. However, that should not mean that the element of human suffering be ignored altogether. The Kashmiris, in over a decade of insurgency, have been subjected to an unprecedented amount of agony and anguish. The agony is obvious as the guilty as well as the innocents both are getting tortured, maimed and killed either at the hands of the insurgents or at the hands of what is sometimes a brutal and insolent soldiery. The anguish finds expression with some difficulty as they have to endure even the rapes and molestation inflicted upon their women, and the sight of children getting orphaned. In effect every man in Kashmir with a gun in his hand has evolved his own brand of law, and some strange, macabre sense of justice is sought to be satisfied as the bullets whiz past both the sides with the average Kashmiri caught in the crossfire. It should also not be lost sight of that the violence in Kashmir has led to the migration of over 50,000 Hindu families from the valley to refugee camps in Jammu and Delhi where they are surviving in the most miserable circumstances.

This research has been undertaken to expose the truth. The people have a right to know that the situation in Kashmir has been (mis) handled in such a manner that it has become a bottomless pit where billions of the hard earned money of the taxpayers have been consumed in internal security duty alone. It should be illuminating to note that the cost of maintaining the 600 companies of the para-military forces last year alone was Rs. 3,634 crore! Readers should find it easy to make a guess about the money which must have been spent on maintaining the three corps of the army and the scores of Rashtriya Rifles battalions. And that is not the end of it. It is a matter of common knowledge that we have provided billions of rupees to the state of Kashmir by way of central assistance for its development. It needs no particular enlightenment to surmise that the motive was, in a way, to appease the Kashmiris so that the level of their alienation with India is reduced and the fever of sedition is brought under control. Certainly there are more ways of killing a cat than choking her with cream! We have not been able to achieve our purpose as a very sizeable fraction of the central assistance was meticulously siphoned off by corrupt politicians and bureaucrats. As far as the alienation part is concerned, it is a highly subjective matter. While it is true that the democratic process has been restored, the fact remains that still any excess committed by the security forces sparks off spontaneous protests in which seditious slogans once again rend the air. The people at large are actually tired of violence–they are tired of the guns of the insurgents, but they are equally tired of the so-called 'crackdowns' of the security forces also. The average Kashmiri is tired of the past; sick of the present and uncertain of the future. When the violence started in 1988, the initial response of the administration was so poor that the opportunist elements in the population thought that the end was near. That is how it assumed the shape of an insurgency. However, as the years passed, the innate weaknesses of the insurgents severely limited the progress of the movement and the euphoria of the opportunist section soon wore off. Obviously the Kashmiris were not psychologically prepared for a long drawn out struggle.

Sometimes it so happens that things take some particularly unpleasant turn and it becomes quite apparent that the responsibility of the *ad hoc* policies pursued heretofore is inescapable. Then they start speaking in terms of evolving a national consensus on Kashmir. However, the very idea of a national consensus remains meaningless unless there is a reasonable degree of national awareness about the matter. One of the purposes of the research presented in the following pages is to create this awareness. It is imperative that the people at large know as to how things have come to such a pass in Kashmir, what we are doing there now, and what do we propose to do in the future. Let us not forget that a safe future can be guaranteed only when the past and the present are analysed objectively for the rights and the wrongs done. In this connection we consider it our duty to point out that journalists have done a great disservice to the people of the nation by presenting a highly fragmented and misleading picture of the developments in Kashmir. In the first place their interests are strictly ephemeral in character. They become interested only when something sensational takes place, and then they proceed to highlight only that fragment. It does not serve the purpose of a journalist to write a small thesis on the subject because then the element of spice is lost. Secondly, they simply do not have the required professional and technical knowledge to understand the intricacies of insurgency and counterinsurgency operations. We have ourselves seen senior army officers describing bags of fertiliser grade ammonium nitrate as highly sophisticated explosive, and the journalists reporting it *verbatim*. The recovery of a third-rate Darrah-made (Darrah–a town near Peshawar) pistol is reported as a deadly foreign-made pistol. The fact is that in a situation like Kashmir, journalists depend to a great extent on the hospitality of the army and the intelligence agencies, who supply them with their versions of the developments. Journalists have only to adorn the text with a couple of photographs and lace it with some racy phrases to create an attractive feature which is, in reality, gloriously false. Let it not be forgotten that the army, the para-military forces and the intelligence agencies have their vested as well as organisational interests in presenting a deliberately distorted picture.

The Role of Hari Singh

The beginning of the muddle in Kashmir can easily be traced to the opportunism of Hari Singh, the then Maharaja of Kashmir. He wanted the best of both worlds. The irony of fate was that he ultimately ended getting the worst of both. He refused to join either India or Pakistan. He was very much apprehensive that Jinnah would dethrone him for religious reasons; at the same time–he hated Nehru for his socialist proclivities and democratic demands. Caught between the two, he decided that 'masterly' inaction was the best policy. Thus he vacillated and procrastinated till a sudden and unwanted turn of events became a *force majeure* for him to take the plunge. In this connection Sardar Patel and Menon have also been blamed for not having taken sufficient interest in the matter of Kashmir despite its having been the third largest princely state after Hyderabad and Mysore. It so alleged that Patel had his personal misgivings about keeping a Muslim majority border state and, in his mind, he had written off Kashmir. As far as Menon is concerned, it may be recalled that Hari Singh had sought to negotiate 'Standstill Agreements' with both the countries. While Pakistan had accepted the proposal. India had rejected it. When the question of this rejection was raised before Menon he said that he simply had no time to think of Kashmir.

Hari Singh wallowed in his indecision till the Pakistanis engineered the infamous raid of the tribals on October 22, 1947. This raid was mounted by a force about 5,000 strong and consisting of Afridi, Wazir, Masud and Swati tribals with a sprinkling of regular Pak army soldiers officially on leave. The force was led by Pak army officers. Except armour and artillery, they had practically all the paraphernalia of a regular infantry like machine guns, mines, wireless sets, etc. As their mobility was ensured by about 250 assorted vehicles, the raiders made a fairly rapid advance. The ill-equipped State troops of Hari Singh were essentially ceremonial in character and were, in any case, spread all over the state. The raiders easily overwhelmed them and by October 26 they reached Baramulla which is 47 km from Srinagar. The raiders were an indisciplined lot and wasted a considerable time in their pursuit of rape and rapine. Otherwise there was a good chance that Srinagar would have fallen. Hari Singh had become aware of the attack only on October 24 when the raiders damaged the Mohora Power Station plunging Srinagar into darkness. He lost no time at all in scooting off to Jammu along with his cars and valuables, leaving the Kashmir Valley like an orphan. It was under such pressing circumstances that he eventually signed the Instrument of Accession on October 26.

Delhi Agreement

The first general election in Jammu and Kashmir after its accession was held in October 1951. In this election, all the 75 Assembly seats were won by the ruling National Conference (NC) led by Sheikh Abdullah. In fact, as many as 73 candidates of the NC were returned unopposed when the nominations closed. The NC candidates were obliged to defeat two independent candidates on the remaining two seats. This was the first link in the chain of frauds that was to beset the state for a very long time. The Assembly elected in this manner constituted itself into a Constituent Assembly. This Constituent Assembly went on to draft a Constitution for the state. It also formally ratified the state's accession to India.

On July 24, 1952 the Government of India entered into an agreement with the government of Sheikh Abdullah. The agreement is known as the Delhi Agreement. Among other things, it provided for the following commitments:

1. That Article 370 would stay.
2. That the Sadar-i-Riyasat (Governor) of the state would be elected by the Legislature and not nominated by the centre.
3. That Emergency in the state could be imposed only with the concurrence of the Legislature.
4. That the advantages given to the State Subjects (natives of the state) earlier would continue.

Sheikh Abdullah's Role

Sheikh Abdullah's only *forte* was the arousing speeches he could deliver. He was a perfect demagogue and never bothered himself with reason. In fact he was so inconsistent in his public utterances that his contemporaries like P.N. Bazaz described him very aptly as a nationalist by day and a communalist by night. It was seriously apprehended in Delhi that his private views were very different from his public pronouncements. In any case, before August 1953, Sheikh Abdullah had started making such irresponsible statements which were sufficient to alarm the Government of India. For example, once he said that Kashmir should have the sympathy of both India and Pakistan, and that it was not necessary that the state should become an appendage of either India or Pakistan. On another occasion he insisted that there was no middle line between full integration and full autonomy, and he wanted the latter.

It is alleged that with the obvious intention of diluting the influence of Sheikh Abdullah, Delhi was cultivating the moderates in the NC like Bakshi Ghulam Mohammed. Sheikh Abdullah was quite apprehensive about it and was even prepared to put Bakshi and his friends behind bars. Meanwhile, there were many more problems for the Government. A respected leader like Shyama Prasad Mukherjee had unfortunately died in custody in Srinagar following his arrest for trying to enter Jammu and Kashmir in the course of this agitation over various issues including the state of Kashmir. It appears that the Government of India had made up its mind to deliver the *coup de maitre* against Sheikh Abdullah so as to cut him down to size once and for all. All it needed was convincing pretext. The pretext was provided by some actions of the Sheikh himself. On August 6, 1953 he asked one of the friends of Bakshi, one Saraf to resign. It is alleged that Saraf refused to resign at the behest of Dr. Karan Singh, the then Sadar-i-Riyasat. It is also alleged that Dr. Karan Singh was in collusion with Delhi. Saraf's refusal led to a piquant situation. Then on August 8, Sheikh Abdullah suddenly went for a trip to Gulmarg. It is alleged that the intelligence agencies convinced the Government that he had gone to meet some Pakistani agent. The Government considered it enough to see to it that Sheikh Abdullah was dismissed on August 9 itself by the Sadar-i-Riyasat. In his place Bakshi was invited to form the government.

Sheikh Abdullah was arrested at Gulmarg. The so-called Pakistani agent was, of course, not to be found anywhere. The Sheikh's arrest and dismissal were followed by widespread disturbances throughout the state and it took about three weeks to control the situation. About 60 people lost their lives in the process. Exactly two years later his trusted lieutenant Mirza Afzal Beig formed the organisation known as the Plebiscite Front. As the name itself suggested, this organisation marked a distinct hardening of the stand taken by the supporters of Sheikh Abdullah. The main demands of he Front were the holding of a plebiscite and the unconditional release of the Sheikh.

Readers should find it singularly edifying to note that though Sheikh Abdullah was dismissed from a constitutional position and arrested apparently on charges of seditious activities, he was not brought to trial for five years. This should provide a classic example of the most cavalier manner in which the politicians had proceeded in matters pertaining to potentially insurgent situations, be it Kashmir, Nagaland or Mizoram. On January 8, 1958 Sheikh Abdullah was released as unceremoniously as he was arrested. We believe that this release was strictly a *ballon d'essai* to watch the behaviour of the Sheikh and not the result of some well-considered policy. About four months later, Sheikh Abdullah was again arrested on April 30, 1958. This arrest became famous as the so-called Kashmir Conspiracy Case, the inspiration for which came apparently from some vague memory of the Meerut Conspiracy Case of the freedom struggle.

Election was held in Jammu and Kashmir in June 1977. The NC under Sheikh Abdullah got a comfortable majority–the Congress and the Janata Party were routed. A suitably appeased Sheikh Abdullah enjoyed power for three years without getting involved in any controversy. In 1980, after Mrs. Gandhi was back in power, the Congress became ambitious and started its machinations so as to gain a foothold in the politics of the state. An agitated Sheikh again started making statements against the Centre. In any case the Sheikh passed away in September, 1982 leaving his son Farooq to carry on the legacy. Initially Farooq also tried to act tough. He raked up the so-called Resettlement Bill by which any Kashmiri subject could return to Kashmir and claim his property. It is believed that Mrs. Gandhi had to engineer some secret understanding with Farooq–the Bill was eventually passed but not implemented. It was not long before Farooq was introduced to the slippery world of *machtpolitik* in a most unpleasant manner. The dark horse turned out to be his own brother-in-law G. M. Shah.

Communal Sensitivity in Kashmir

Unlike several other parts of the country, Kashmir had never exhibited a very high degree of communal sensitivity in the past. Hence the communal violence of February-March 1986 ought not to be dismissed as an aberration. In fact it was a manifestation of the fact that the fundamentalist and communal forces which had been obliged to keep a low profile heretofore, had succeeded in gaining wider acceptability and that too at the cost of the so-called secular forces represented by the regular political system. It should be quite interesting to note that in the initial phase fundamentalism and communalism went *pari passu* with the secessionist sentiments. For the 1987 election various fundamentalist and communal organisations like the Ummat-e-Islami, Tahafuz-ul-Islam, Muslim Employees Front and Islamic Students League, etc. formed a political conglomerate called the Muslim United Front (MUF). The influential J&K Jamat-e-Islami (lEI) also lost no time in joining it. Besides their obvious preference for a position with a distinct communal skew, their political plank was that the NC had committed a moral crime by allying with the Congress for the sake of power and that in the process they had bartered the special identity of the state.

The results of the 1987 election came as a shock to most Kashmiris. The NC-Congress combine had bagged 66 seats. The MUF could get only four and that too when it had secured 31 per cent of the votes polled in the Valley. In fact the MUF and the People's Conference put together had secured about 50 per cent of the votes polled. Although it is well known that legendary fraud was committed in this election and all sorts of electoral malpractices were resorted to, the very fact that the MUF had got 31 per cent of the votes polled in the Valley must be a clear indicator of its popularity at that time. Simultaneously, it is also an indication of the degree of subversion and the degree of arousal of the Muslim sentiments. As expected, there were immediate and widespread allegations of rigging and misuse of power by the state against its political opponents in various forms. It was found that hundreds of opposition workers had been arrested in advance. Booth capturing was also reported. Some people had seen bundles of ballot papers already stamped for the NC-Congress candidates lying in the polling booths. A large number of votes cast in the favour of MUF candidates were invalidated on technical grounds, such as the ink/stamp being smudged. The bungling did not stop at that. Once the counting began, several areas of the Valley were placed under declared or undeclared curfew. The idea was to prevent people from taking to the streets once the results were declared. In fact, in several constituencies where the MUF candidates were leading, counting was kept suspended for as much as a week. At several places, the opposition candidates were thrown out of the counting centres. To cap the lot, most of the MUF leaders were arrested later.

The 1987 election left it far behind. It turned out to be the proverbial last straw. The Sheikh could afford to be inconsistent and irrational for he had an immense appeal amongst the general masses. It must be admitted that the Kashmir psyche has always had shades of isolationism and an ambivalent attitude towards India with a compulsive tendency to blame Delhi for almost everything. That popular sentiments were fired to a large extent by such an attitude was regularly and convincingly reflected in the response of the people to the anti-India or anti-Centre fulminations of Sheikh Abdullah. Still it did not manifest itself in the form of an armed insurrection. Even if the people were getting disillusioned with the political system, the charismatic personality of the Sheikh held them from slipping into an inexorable slide. No such restraining device was available after the 1987 election. The alliance of the National Conference with the Congress and their conduct of the elections made the NC lose a great deal of its credibility among the masses. Since the NC had dominated the political scene of the state for so long, its loss of credibility created a sort of political vacuum in the state. This vacuum was promptly filled in by the fundamentalist, communal and secessionist forces. Any society has always a large number of people who are normally non-committed but are prone to be swayed in any direction. This section of the society and the lot which was already subverted started according some sort of general approval to the unconstitutional means of protest adopted by the fundamentalist and secessionist forces. As anguish turn into anger it was only a matter of time that the guns appeared on the scene.

The situation underwent a qualitative change in 1989. The number of insurgents who had their training in POK or Pakistan went up. At the same time they were supplied with a larger number of AK rifles and explosives. In 1989 the insurgents thought it best to impart the flavour of popular movement to their activities. Moreover they also lent a distinct communal hue to their reactions. For accomplishing the former they organised a series of agitations and strikes. The pretexts ranged from observing January 26 as 'black day' to the death anniversary of Maqbool Butt; from protest against the book 'Satanic Verses' to the call for 'Quit Kashmir'; from observing August 15 as 'black day' to the dealth anniversary of Gen. Zia; from the dealth anniversary of JKLF insurgent Aijaz Ahmed Dar to protest against the arrest of Shabir Ahmed Shah on September 28; and finally to remember with grief the day when the Indian forces had first entered Kashmir in 1947 that is, October 27.

To accomplish the latter, threatening letters were posted to non-Kashmiris in general and Hindus in particular asking them to leave the Valley. They also started attacks on the Hindus and their property. Simultaneously, the JEI (J&K) and its front organisations like the Hizb-e-Islami and Hizb-e-Mujahideen, etc. started a reform movement in the practice of Islam in Kashmir with a heavy bias in favour of the most orthodox.

It was in such an atmosphere that the 1989 general election was announced. Almost all the secessionist groups gave a call for a boycott of the polls. As a result, complete strike was observed throughout the Valley on November 22 and 24. The percentage of polling in the two constituencies (Baramulla and Anantnag) where elections were held was just about 5 per cent, reducing this election also into a farce. From the point of view of studying insurgency, it is important to note that the tremendous response to the call of the boycott of the polls was a clear and unambiguous demonstration of the sway which the secessionists had come to hold over the general public.

Change in the Activities of the Insurgents

By the end of 1990 a definite and characteristic pattern had emerged in the activities of the insurgents. Firstly, the mosques had become very important platforms and the Maulvis very important tools for the dissemination of subversive propaganda. Secondly, the internationalisation of the issues was sought to be achieved by ensuring that almost all demonstrations ended up by submitting memoranda to the U.N. Military Observer Group's office in Srinagar. Thirdly, political activists and their properties were made into special targets of violence. A series of political assassinations ensured that there was complete panic among their ranks, and gradually all sorts of political activities came to a grinding halt. It also signified the fact that the insurgency had gained sufficient momentum of its own and it no longer needed the backing of the cadres of any political party. It should, therefore, not be surprising that the Mir Waiz Maulvi Farooq himself was killed by the insurgents on May 21. They derived some mileage out of even that as there were disturbances during the federal procession of the Mir Waiz, and the police firing had left about 30 people dead providing fresh fuel for the anti-government sentiments. Fourthly, in order to ensure a thorough demoralisation among those government employees who were still with India, they selectively killed about 170 government employees. Fifthly, the insurgents introduced the element of a virulent communalisation of their violence. The number of Hindus killed in the year went up to 177. That is enough to trigger the exodus of about 40,000 Hindu and 1,500 Sikh families from the Valley.

The pattern of insurgent activities remained essentially the same in 1991 also. As they gained some experience, the insurgents became more daring in their attacks on the security forces and senior officers. On June 1, 1991 the convoy of the DGP of the state was ambushed. Even in such a situation somebody had sold the idea of holding talks with the insurgents in an attempt to achieve a diplomatic *coup de maitre*! Luckily it turned out to be a *coup manque* instead as the insurgents set quite impossible terms for the talks–Shabir Shah demanded that the talks be held in Geneva! '

Even more daring attacks were witnessed in 1992. There was a massive explosion in the Police Headquarters, which left the DGP and five other very senior officers seriously injured. It should be obvious that the insurgents had been able to achieve such a high degree of subversion in the police that they could plant a bomb in the Police Headquarters itself. Another sensational incident was that of a land-mine explosion in the route of the Adviser to the Governor, and the DGP. It should be easily discernible that this was possible only when someone had passed the information regarding their movement on a certain route to the insurgents. In this year some political mileage was sought to be achieved by the farcical drama of the so-called 'Ekta Yatra' of the BJP. That it was a burlesque attempt was exposed the moment all sorts of pretexts and excuses were found for the 'Yatra' to be airlifted to Srinagar so as to avoid travelling by road in the Valley. However, the real opprobrium lay in the fact that some people considered it an achievement to hoist the national flag at Lal Chowk, Srinagar on the Republic Day! The people of the nation should hang their heads in shame if the politicians had allowed an insurgency to attain such dimensions that it was considered unsafe to hoist the national flag in the main market of the capital of one of our states on the Republic Day!

By 1992 the Pakistani involvement in the insurgency in Kashmir had reached such a level that they had a sufficiently large number of insurgents who were totally in consonance with the Pakistani line of thought on Kashmir. Hence, they were no longer obliged to support an organisation like the JKLF which demanded an independent nation of Kashmir. Thus started the process of margination of the JKLF by the Pakistani agencies. This explains the refusal by the Pakistani authorities when Amanullah Khan wanted to cross the LOC in a dramatic 'march to Kashmir on February 11 and again on March 30. That the JKLF has still been allowed to exist on the soil of POK and operate from there is only an act of abundant prudence to take care of any unforeseen developments or an unexpected turn of events in Kashmir.

The insurgents, with the active support of Pakistan, were able to maintain a fairly high and roughly constant level of violence as well as subversion for four more years. The level of subversion has certainly gone down since then as most people admitted the futility of the venture. As a result, the insurgency passed into the stage of terrorism.

Terrorist Organisations in Kashmir

Hizb-ul-Mujahideen (HUM)

This outfit was created in September 1989 in Pakistan. The first chief of the outfit was Master Ahsan Dar. Because of the involvement of the Pak JEI, the JEI (J&K) also readily extended its patronage to the HUM. At an ideological level the HUM derives its inspiration from the JEI. It is due to the JEI inspired stress on fundamentalism that many insurgents call it a *'deen pasant tanzeem'* (faith loving outfit). The HUM had greatly benefited in the past and still benefit from the extensive network of the dedicated cadres of the JEI. The JEI cadres and the clergy are largely responsible for subverting the boys and recruiting them for terrorism.

The strength of the HUM cadres is estimated to be in the vicinity of 1,500.

Harkat-ul-Ansar (HUA)

This is an international terrorist organisation. It is because of its international features that the USA was ultimately forced to declare it a terrorist organisation. The HUA has got its branches in several other countries also. The HUA was formed in December 1993 by the merger of two outfits, namely, the Harkat-ul-Mujahideen and the Harkat-ul-Jehad-e-Islami. The Harkat-ul-Mujahideen was an old organisation in Pakistan formed with the express purpose of preparing the youth for taking part in the war in Afghanistan. In that war it was associated with an Afghan Mujahideen group called Zameel-e-al-Hadisi. After things became rather cold in Afghanistan, they turned their attention elsewhere. In 1989 they opened a branch in Domel, POK. By 1990 they developed some interest in Kashmir and one Sajjad Afghani was despatched to Kashmir to establish a branch of the organisation there. The Harkat-ul-Jehad-e-Islami, on the other hand, was formed by Maulana Irshad and Maulana Khalid Zubair in Karachi. The Kashmir unit of this outfit was started in 1991 through one Maulavi Jamshed.

After the formation of the HUA in 1993 its chief (Amir-e-Aala) is one Maulana Fazl-ul-Rehman Khalil, a resident of Dera Ismail Khan, Pakistan. Its important leaders in Kashmir are Maulana Farooq Kashmiri and Hatf Bhai. The strength of the HUA terrorists in Kashmir is believed to be around 800.

The HUA has always had an eye on gaining a status of notoriety quite disproportionate to its real capability. It was for this reason that they had 'banned' the 'Amarnath Yatra,' knowing well that a cancellation of the 'Yatra' due to terrorist threat would make for an immense loss of face for the Government. Although in practice they could do nothing more than cause a couple of explosions on the route, the Government was obliged to make excessively heavy security arrangements for the 'Yatra,' inflicting an enormous strain on the security forces and a huge expenditure as well. It is also believed that the HUA was responsible for the kidnapping of the foreigners in July 1995 under the pseudonym of a hitherto unknown outfit called 'Al Faran.' The belief is reinforced by the fact that the group Al Faran was not heard of after that incident. HUA terrorists have got the advantage of having a predominant component of foreign mercenaries among their ranks. Thus they do not have any stakes in local disputes and rivalries, saving them a considerable amount of energy and resources.

Lashkar-e-Taiba (LET)

The Lashkar-e-Taiba is the armed wing of an Islamic fundamentalist organisation called Markaz-e-Dawat-ul-Irshad based in Pakistan. However, a great deal of the logistic support is provided by the ISI. The Markaz-e-Dawat-ul-Irshad was formed way back in the early 1980s at Muridke, Pakistan, under the patronage of the Jamiat Ahl-e-Hadis (Hafiz Mohammed Yahya group). The Markaz had been closely associated with the ISI in the days of the Afghan War. Because of the legacy of patronage by the Ahl-e-Hadis sect which is avowedly pan-Islamic in character, the Markaz has had close links with Ahl-e-Hadis groups elsewhere in the world, particularly in Saudi Arabia and Sudan. It has also got links with other international Muslim terrorist organisations including the Ikhwan-ul Musalmeen of Egypt, the Islamic radical groups of

Algeria and the Arab guerrilla groups. In Egypt there is an organisation called Al-Gama-al-Islamia.

Tehrik-e-Jehad (TEJ)

The Tehrik-e-Jehad is one of the latest terrorist outfits floated by the ISI in April 1997. It is strongly suspected that the TEJ has been formed with the basic intention of side-stepping the declaration of the HUA as a terrorist organisation by the USA. Now the same activities may be carried out by the terrorists without the risk of any sanctions or embarrassment to the Pak Government. This outfit is manned exclusively by mercenaries. In POK, Sardar Abdul Qayoom (ex-MP, Muslim Conference) has extended his patronage to the TEJ. It is believed that the TEJ has got about 250 terrorists in Kashmir.

In addition to the HUM, HUA, LET and TEJ there are still at least nine smaller outfits active in Kashmir. The important ones among them are Al Jehad Force, Al Barq and J&K Muslim Mujahideen.

The Al Jehad Force was created in December 1991. It can be regarded as the armed wing of the political party called People's League. The People's League had given birth to several groups, namely, the Muslim Janbaz Force, the Kashmir Jehad Force and the Al Fateh Force.

Kul Jamat Hurriyat Conference(KJHC)

The KJHC is a heterogeneous agglomerate of as many as 30 fundamentalist organisations and secessionist groups and parties. It was formed in March 1993. The secessionists felt that it would be better to have a single body which could represent them all. The ulterior motive was that if at all they had to negotiate with the Government of India at some point of time, a single body would negotiate better. Also, they thought that it would pre-empt any argument of the Government of India that it would not negotiate where a multiplicity of groups with diverse ideologies and demands claimed to represent the will of the Kashmiri people. Moreover, the insurgents considered it advantageous to have somewhat more respectable people to represent them and who could articulate things in a relatively better way. Such people include advocates and a retired Chief Justice of the J&K High Court. In practice the KJHC turned out to be so badly beset by internal dissensions and personality clashes that it could never command the respect of the people even when seditious sentiment ran high. In the absence of a unifying stream of thought, the constituents of the KJHC could achieve unanimity only for giving calls for strikes–no wonder the people have nicknamed it the 'hartal conference'! Furthermore, ever since insurgency in Kashmir regressed to terrorism, the ISI also has lost interest in the KJHC, though they have not abandoned the control of its key leaders so that they could be used to deal with any unexpected development.

The present chairman of the KJHC is Abdul Ghani Butt, originally of the Muslim Conference. The presently active terrorist groups do not attach any significance to the KJHC as the ISI is, at the moment, not interested in any negotiations but wants to continue terrorism to bleed India. For them the contextual relevance of the KJHC is satisfied by its incessant harping on the alleged violations of human rights at various fora. Thus, in our opinion, we do not stand the chance of achieving anything substantial even if the KJHC is inclined for some agreement–the ISI would not only ridicule any agreement, they may also step up the violence in retaliation. Furthermore, it would impart a label of importance to the KJHC, which it really does not deserve through its support base among the people. In fact a more strident need of the hour would be to devise counter-measures for the blackmailing of the National Conference by the KJHC into adopting a stance characterised by regressive induration.

Facing of Terrorism in Kashmir

It is so very important to appreciate that in spite of the insurgency having regressed to a state of terrorism, the strike potential of the terrorists has not diminished at all. There should still be about 3,500–4,000 terrorists in Kashmir. The porosity of the LOC/border is still as glaring as ever. As a result of this the ISI is eminently capable of replenishing the losses inflicted upon the terrorists by the security forces. The terrorists have now a much higher percentage of foreign mercenaries among their ranks. The mercenaries are better motivated on account of religious fanaticism, do not show a propensity to get involved in inter-group clashes, and are better fighters. There has been some qualitative improvement in their weaponry also as weapons like Automatic Grenade Launchers are also found being used. Some heavy machine guns are also available. Though explosives were available earlier also, now there is a more skilful use of IEDs and mines. In general it is seen that the attacks on the security forces have become deadlier and more daring with some of them bordering on the suicidal. This can be attributed to the higher professional skill of the mercenaries. Further, though the general level of subversion has gone down substantially, the terrorists are still able to manage the necessary shelter either by coercion or by invoking the Universal Islamic Brotherhood. Unlike the Sikh terrorists, in Kashmir we do not hear of many excesses committed by the mercenaries on the local population, particularly in terms of the violation of their womenfolk. A rather disturbing trend is the extension of the terrorist activities to the Jammu region, particularly Doda district, where they find it easier to disappear into the spacious hills. In these areas they have once again started selective killings of Hindus so as to impart a communal colour to their activities. If these killings provoke a communal backlash, that too would be of help to them. Firstly, the resultant deterioration in the public order situation would place undue stress on the police, making its vigil weaker elsewhere, and rendering them more prone to terrorist strikes. Secondly, they hope to induce a favourable disposition in the Muslim community in case some of them happen to suffer at the hands of the police or the Hindus. Further, by virtue of its populous nature and the extent of development, the Jammu region lends itself easily to acts of sabotage and pure terrorism. These could include explosions at crowded public places, sabotage of railway property and strikes on essential services like electricity and water supply–these are only a few illustrative examples; the possible targets are limited only by the ingenuity of the terrorists.

The Terrorist Violence

On analysing the figures for terrorist violence we find that as far as the civilian targets are concerned, the attacks had reached a prominent peak in 1996. This is quite understandable as the insurgents were making a last-ditch effort to stall the political process. During the period 1994–1999, civilian targets were attacked at an average rate of 774 attacks per year. In 1999, it had come to 658 or so. Similarly, about 776 civilians were being killed per year on an average for 1994–1999. In 1999, it was about 541 per year. The number of civilians injured also came down from the average of 991 to 791.

Attacks on the security forces tell a different story altogether. There has been a distinct reduction in the number of attacks on the security forces. However the casualties inflicted have actually gone up! The average figures for 1994-1999 were 187 killed and 534 injured per year, giving a total casualty figure of 721 per year. In 1999 it rose to 751 per year (264 killed and 487 injured) in spite of the fact that the number of attacks in 1999 had come down to 1,021 from the yearly average of 1,568. This analysis is a clear indication of the fact that the terrorists are now proceeding about their business in a more systematic manner. The attacks are better planned and executed in a more professional way as a result of which the lethality of the attacks has improved by as much as 61 per cent, that is, now 61 per cent more casualties are being inflicted per attack. This could be attributed partially to the increased induction of more proficient mercenaries. On a tactical plane this translates into progressively abandoning the romance of amateurish fire from the AK in favour of the somewhat cowardly but more effective use of land-mines/IEDs. It also indicates that they are becoming more proficient in selecting the targets.

As for as counterinsurgency operations are concerned, we find that in the period 1994-99 terrorists were killed at an average rate of 1,104 per year. In fact the peak was in 1994 itself and it has been continuously going down since then. The figure for 1999 was 685, that is down by 38 per cent from the average. A similar but more severe slide is noticed in the case of arrests of the terrorists also. The average figure for the number of arrests in one year was, 2,466. In 1999 it came down to 658, that is, down by 73 per cent. This trend can be partially attributed to a slackening of the pace of the anti-terrorist drive, which almost inevitably follows the installation of a popular government; the security forces certainly feel more free to operate during President's Rule. Further, with the local recruitment process having got slowed down greatly, the attrition in the ranks of the terrorists is also partly responsible for it. Exfiltration of the local boys is very much reduced now; however; it is estimated that infiltration of the mercenaries still takes place at the rate of about 600 to 1,000 per year. With the installation of the popular government it was considered *de rigueur* to stage-manage a large number of surrenders. We do not attach any significance to such dramas–there were occasions when either the terrorists covered their faces or the same faces were seen at more than one function. In any case, the number of such surrenders in 1999 was just 56. The very concept of surrender had some relevance in the insurgency phase; once the phase of terrorism controlled by an external agency has come to stay, the surrender of some offender of yesteryears has the same significance as a corpse coming back to life and dying again–at best he could be interested in the post-surrender benefits doled out by the administration and in nothing else.

Readers must get a clear idea of the present level of violence in Kashmir. There are still over three attacks on the security forces per day in Kashmir inflicting over two casualties in killed and injured–about 10 such attacks leave 13 to 14 security forces personnel dead or injured. At least two civilian targets are still being struck per day causing a daily casualty of about four persons. Almost every second day there is some bomb/IED/grenade explosion somewhere. On the other hand the rate of neutralisation of the terrorists comes to about four per day in terms of killed and arrested. While forming a mental picture of the state of terrorism, the readers should never lose sight of the fact that the Kashmir Valley has only six districts in it with an area of just over 15,000 sq. km and an estimated population of just over 40 lakhs. The gravity of the problem can be properly appreciated only in such a correct perspective.

Terrorists and Our Nation

It may be recalled that not only the wearing of masks, but the whole manner in which the terrorists treated this great nation of ours was demeaning. The offer itself smacked of condescension which, in any way, did not befit a group of terrorists. Their insistence on not surrendering before the talks, and setting their own terms for the dialogue were calculated acts of insult. The insult was completed by the gruffness which they showed in calling off the cease-fire. The message which they were trying to convey to us and to the world was that they were going to do us a big favour and we, out of our obstinacy, blew it up. This episode, therefore, deserves a closer analysis. We will first examine the open information. Then we will, for the sake of completeness, describe the speculation that was made in the media, hinting that the whole thing was a result of back channel diplomacy or an intelligence operation. Readers must keep in mind that Abdul Majid Dar, by making such an announcement had succeeded in assuming an aura of legitimacy. Dar and his group are not a sovereign nation at war with us. He had, therefore, no right to announce a cease-fire. As far as the legal position is concerned, they are all criminals accused of having committed the most heinous offences. And criminals do not oblige a sovereign State by declaring a cease-fire or suspension of their criminal activities. At this juncture, let us make it very clear that, one of us being a serving officer, we are neither commenting on the wisdom of the Government's policy of holding the talks nor criticising it in any way. If the Government thought it proper to have a dialogue, so be it, and let us hope for the best. We are only making the legal and moral positions clear from a purely academic angle so that the development may be seen in its proper perspective. In such situations anywhere in the world, the criminals do not acquire a right to demand or claim a dialogue with a sovereign State unless they first surrender before the law of the State. Dar assumed for himself a *de facto* position which he or his group had no right to possess. Further, it must be kept in mind that there is no reason to believe that the HUM or the faction led by Dar represented all the terrorists who had taken up arms against the State. In fact, there were several other outfits which had scoffed at the offer and went on to convey their 'displeasure' by murdering about 100 innocent civilians on a single day even as the 'peace talks' were going on. This was an extremely serious affront to the authority of the State, calling for the most exemplary punishment. From a purely practical angle also, the cease-fire by a single group or faction would have posed enormous difficulties before the security forces. There was no way in which the security forces could have made out that a certain terrorist was from the HUM or not unless they were carrying some sort of ID or had agreed to move out of Kashmir for that period. According to the open information, Dar had not made any such offer. We fully endorse the Government's stand of not holding any tripartite talks involving Pakistan. It was very much in keeping with our standard line. To do otherwise might well have negated the enormous price which we have paid in the past decade in terms of money, human life and suffering.

Once again, this episode left a lesson for the counterinsurgency fighters. In this business there are no short cuts; there is nothing which can substitute for sustained hard work. Let no one delude himself into believing that in counterinsurgency one could stage a diplomatic *coup de maitre* and finish it in one stroke. Perhaps we should have remembered and learnt from the fiasco of February 1991 when the insurgents had set impossible terms for the talks. This episode had a disconcerting fallout also. We have ascertained that the message as perceived by the people and the terrorists at the end of the day was that we were eager to talk to the HUM because the security forces had failed in bringing them to their knees. Thus a boost in the morale of the terrorists was indeed noticeable. Further, they were happy that, in the process, they had once again succeeded, as they had at the time of the Kargil conflict, in bringing the Kashmir issue back into international focus. It should be pointed out that, in such a situation, if some people had been hoping that they could drive a wedge between the local and the foreign (mercenary) insurgents and thus isolate the latter for eventual attrition, we must say that they were sadly mistaken. In fact this betrays a poor understanding of the phenomenon of terrorism in Kashmir. Perhaps it needs to be understood that terrorism in Kashmir is no longer a spontaneous phenomenon. It is being sustained from across the border under a masterly plan and they would be able to execute it to a satisfactory degree even if the local boys are not with them. It needs to be appreciated that such a phenomenon cannot be defeated merely by some operations of a kind that would intend to generate some internal dissensions amongst the ranks of the terrorists. May be we can wean away a couple of leaders or even an entire faction. But these will remain purely temporary setbacks to the movement. In such situations, terrorist movements, and particularly those sustained from across the border, are able to recover rather quickly by reorganising themselves.

There were many conjectures in the media about the covert part of it. It was hinted that it was an intelligence operation and Abdul Majid Dar had been cultivated. It was also alleged that Dar had made a secret visit to Delhi where he had met senior RAW and IB officers. It was also pointed out that Dar had taken a commercial flight from Dubai to New Delhi before emplaning for Srinagar without being halted en route by Indian authorities, and that itself indicated that his travel plans had been worked out in advance. For obvious reasons, we decline to comment on such conjectures. Several things are possible. It is not unlikely that, for some reason, Dar wants to come overground like Yasin Malik, Shabir Shah and Kuka Parrey, and dabble in politics. It is also possible that there was some miscalculation in the ISI itself. Perhaps they might have expected that India would never accept the HUM cease-fire offer. Perhaps Dar became more ambitious than what he was supposed to be, and the ISI thought it best to scuttle the whole thing before it blossomed into something undesirable for them.

The role of the media in this affair was quite reprehensible. While their happiness in stating that talking is better than warring could be understood, it was amusing to note that they started addressing Dar as Mr. Abdul Majid Dar while still calling Salauddin *sans* the Mister. Dar's masked cronies came to be addressed as Hizbul commanders. It appeared that they were subconsciously trying to convey the impression that Dar was a gentleman whereas Salauddin was not, and that those terrorists were commanders of some formations, which in spite of their dastardly and seditious acts, deserved the respect of the State.

Readers may recall that since November 2000 the Government has declared a unilateral cease-fire in Kashmir. Since it is a matter of a recent policy of the Government, we decline to offer any comment on the policy or its wisdom. However, for the sake of the completeness of the narrative and for the information of the readers we may quote that the cease-fire has been defined in the following words: "The cease fire does not mean that the soldiers will not pick up weapons if attacked by terrorist groups or if there is infiltration from across the border.

5

Political Roots of Terrorism

Violence and American Culture

The first article 'America's Bomb Culture,' by Christopher John Farle, writing in *Time* magazine, analyse the FBI's Bomb Data Centre statistics to establish a correlation between the 'dissemination of bomb know-how' and the rising incidence of actual bombings. In the process, Farley portrays a culture that is all too accommodating to the violence inherent to terrorist activity. The second article, 'Connect the Dots,' by Frank Rich of *The New York Times*, examines the political ideologies of extremist militia groups. Just as Farley, in the first article, strives to link terrorist action with mainstream culture, Rich searches out links between groups with apparently disparate agendas-opponents of gun control, anti-abortion extremists, Christian fundamentalists, white supremacists, and a range of paramilitary militias. At the very least, Rich demonstrates how thin a line can separate gross political and social discontent from a terrorist's rationale.

In a speech given by David B. Kopel, entitled 'The Federal Government Should Set a Better Example,' the increase of federal authority and the perceived violence of federal law enforcement are cited as contributing to the increase in domestic terrorism. Kopel asserts that the best way to defuse the growing American militia movement is to curb the federal government's power and avoid the abusive behaviour that characterized the assault on the Branch-Davidian compound at Waco, Texas, and the siege of Ruby Ridge in Idaho.

Tom Bethell, writing in *The American Spectator,* calls the recent growth in terrorism primarily a reaction to a 'federal government (that) has accumulated too much power, and needs to back off.' In the article entitled 'Turnabout Is Fair Play,' Bethell, arguing in a conservative vein, decries the growth in federal power that has occurred in recent years and theorizes that the increase in national terrorism is related to the Post-World War II expansion of federal authority and the consequent reduction of state power.

Grubisic's experience is reflected in the data collected by the FBI's Bomb Data Centre, which counted 1,880 bombings in 1993, up from 442 a decade earlier. In 1993, bombs killed 43 and injured 281, up from 29 dead and 230 wounded two years earlier. The increase does not take into account the six deaths and 1,042 injuries caused by the 1993 bombing of the World Trade Centre. According to the Bureau of Alcohol, Tobacco and Firearms, about half the bombing attempts in 1993 were acts of vandalism, 13 per cent were intended as revenge and fewer than 1 per cent were acts of protest.

A significant factor in the increase in bombings in that the dissemination of bomb know-how has become a minor industry. The past few decades have produced the rise of mail-order publishing companies that serve the so-called gun aftermarket, including the gun fanciers, survivalists, wannabe cops and closet anarchists who like to shop for such products as laser sights, camouflage, fake badges and fake FBI and ATF hats. Some of their most popular offerings are 'burn-and blow' books that describe in detail how to make land mines, booby traps and bombs. 'The information is available on the Internet and everywhere else,' says retired ATF agent AI Gleason, who spent 50 years investigating bombings. 'People who feel that the bomb might be their weapon of choice now have the information to make one.'

One of the earliest and most successful products of these publishers is the *Anarchist Cookbook*, which was put out in 1971 by Lyle Stuart Inc. But to bomb-squad commanders, the most notorious publisher is Paladin Press in Boulder, Colorado, founded in 1970 by two Special Forces veterans of the Vietnam War. The company carries a catalogue of 40 books and videos on how to make explosives, including the *Improvised Munitions Black Book* series repackaged versions of military manuals with instructions for building explosives. Paladin's list also carries *Homenlade* C-4; *A Recipe for Survival*, about which one catalogue edition says, 'Serious survivors know that the day may come when they need something more powerful than commercial dynamite......For blowing bridges, shattering steel and derailing tanks, they need C-4.'

Burn-and-blow publishers argue that there is no correlation between their material, which often carries the caveat 'for information purposes only,' and the increasing rate of bombings across the nation. 'I sell a thousand books, but there arn't a thousand expiosions,' says Billy Blann, the owner of Delta Press Ltd. of El Dorado, Arkansas. The flurry of orders after the Oklahoma bombing for the pamphlet *Improvised Munitions from Ammonium Nitrate*, he says, is 'just armchair people who want to know what's going on.'

Hollywood too has become fascinated. With gunplay so common in real life, producers have turned to bombers as the villains *du jour*. On TV, the season finale of *Melrose Place* features a character who sets off a bomb at the apartment complex that houses the show's cast. The ABC soap opera *All My Children* contains a story line in which a character has been planning to bomb an ex-lover on his wedding day. In the wake of the Oklahoma bombing, producers of the soap opera say they are altering the bomb angle, while *Melrose Place's* producers are considering the same measure. At the movies, the Chuck Norris film Top *Dog* begins with the bombing of an apartment building by neo-Nazis. Due May 19 is the Bruce Willis thriller *Die Hard with a Vengeance*, which opens with the bombing of a department store. Bombings have been featured in *Speed, Blown Alvay* and *The Specialist*. Moviemakers contend that they are merely reflecting reality.

When the full history of home grown American terrorism in the 1990's is written, the chapter before Oklahoma city will tell of a little-noticed press conference last August in New York.

It was called by Planned Parenthood to showcase a videotape of a meeting held by the Wisconsin branch of the far-right US Taxpayers Party. The meeting's speakers included two of the country's most militant anti-abortion leaders, Randall Terry of Operation Rescue and Matthew Trewhella of Missionaries to the Preborn. But they weren't talking about abortion. Mr. Trewhella spoke of training his young child to use guns. The meeting's attendees were offered a manual titled *'Principles Justifying the Arming and Organizing of a Militia'* in which the *Bible* was invoked to justify the formation 'assault terms' to protect the unborn.

For Planned Parenthood, which had been forced by Reagan Era Federal indifference to do its own research into the steep 1980's rise in abortion-clinic bombings and murder, this demonstrable link between anti-abortion extremists and a growing militia movement was a major breakthrough. In the stepped-up investigation that followed, Planned Parenthood began to uncover a commingling of anti-abortion extremists, new-world-order paranoids, Waco Wackos, Reconstructionist Christians, white supremacists and assault-weapon fanatics in a national paramilitary subculture. Abortion turned out to be merely the come-on issue, designed to attract followers to a rabid anti-government crusade.

Since the Oklahoma bombing, Federal Law Enforcement Officials have been in constant touch with Planned Parenthood, explained Pamela Maraldo, the organization's president. By now they've no doubt seen an anti-abortion terrorism manual from the mid-1980's with an elaborate illustrated plan for building a fertilizer bomb. Presumably, the FBI is also consulting the Southern Poverty Law Centre, the Anti-Defamation League and the American Jewish Committee, which, like Planned Parenthood, were driven by criminality in their own backyards to investigate the paramilitary right. As the Jewish weekly *The Forward* reported anti-Semitic violence in the militia strongholds to Idaho and Montana is now routine.

It's not yet known whether this evidence will connect a specific militia or far-right group of the Oklahoma tragedy. What is clear is how extensively the nation's far-right factions are interconnected, forming a political network that often publicly espouses the same ideology as the terrorists in our midst, much as the Sinn Fein speaks aboveground for the IRA.

For one example of the far-right's cohesiveness, consider Lawrence Pratt, head of the rabid Gun Owners of America. Wearing another hat, Mr. Pratt also runs the Committee to Protect the Family Foundation, a fundraiser for Operation Rescue. As a public speaker, Mr. Pratt tours with 'Preparedness Expo '95,' where he shares top billing with Mark ('From Michigan') Koernke, the short wave radio voice of the militia movement, and Bo Gritz, the Idaho militia guru and Christian Covenant leader who described the Oklahoma bombing as 'a Rembrandt–a masterpiece of science and art put together.'

And who is the biggest recipient of campaign funds from Mr. Pratt's Gun Owners of America? None other than Representative Steve Stockman, the Texas Republican who denied any connection to militias when asked to explain the mysterious fax his office received after the Oklahoma bombing, Even so, *Roll Call*, the Capitol Hill paper, condemned Mr. Stockman and Idaho's Representative Helen Chenoweth on Thursday in an editorial titled 'Paranold Fringe.'

At last, though at a high price, the country and Justice Department are starting to catch up to Planned Parenthood. As Frederick Clarkson, one of its researchers of the radical right, says: "Abortion clinics have had an average of 15 bombings or arsons every year for a decade. If that had happened at churches or newspapers or Federal office buildings, we would have called it terrorism. But society didn't want to recognize the pattern of violence.'

Now that we're starting to recognize the complexity of that pattern, we also see that even when all the Oklahoma City bombing suspects are arrested, the investigation will have only just begun.

Today, there are many tens of millions of people who are frightened of the government, and many thousands (or perhaps more) who participate in militias. Some of them may have incorrect beliefs about the Brady Bill or the ban on so-called 'assault weapons,' or the United Nations, or other political issues. But allegedly mistaken beliefs are no basis for federal jurisdiction.

Within these groups, as there are within almost any other group, are a few criminals. Just as citizens should not imagine that because a few Congress people are found guilty of felonies most Congress people are criminals, Congress people should not imagine that because a few persons with anti-government viewpoints are criminals, many or most militia members or other government critics are criminals.

Let us learn from history. Let us not be panicked into hasty action that history will judge harshly. Let us begin a process of respectful dialogue and reform, not stereotyping and repression.

As Justice Braildeis understood, 'Repression breeds hate; hate menaces stable government; the path of safety lies in the opportunity to discuss freely supposed grievances and proposed remedies.'

One of the reasons that so many people have become fearful of the federal government, and some have become angry, has been the virtually uninterrupted expansion of federal laws, at the expense of civil liberty. The cycle of misleading media sensationalism, a couple of congressional hearings, and then another broad and intrusive federal 'remedy' has become all too familiar.

It is possible to assemble before any given congressional panel a half-dozen very sincere witnesses who will claim that any given topic is:

1. An immense problem;
2. Rapidly spiraling out of control all over the nation; and
3. Desperately in need of an immediate, sweeping federal remedy.

Before enacting additional legislation in an atmosphere of media hype and prejudice, Congress would do well to slow down.

For example, we have no reliable hard data about how often government employees are being threatened or attacked. Still less do we have any hard data about how often existing state and federal laws are inadequate to punish the criminals involved.

Current criminal laws do not require that authorities wait until someone has actually been injured or killed. Making threats is, of course, a crime in itself.

Nor are states necessarily helpless or unwilling to act. In no state are the people who perpetrate or support violent crimes against government officials the majority of the population. Or even close to it.

Some problems are plainly inappropriate for a federal 'solution.' For example, some persons–living proof of the principle that a little knowledge is a dangerous thing have–begun filing purported liens or other alleged 'common law,' instruments in some state courts. Surely the remedy for abuse of state court procedures is through enforcement of existing procedural rules which punish frivolous or false legal filings, or through reforms of state court systems to provide whatever additional remedies may be needed. State courts are the business of the states, not of Congress.

Anti-Government Violence

In regards to anti-government violence, proposals for broad new conspiracy statutes, or for broad new judicial authority to destroy or disband organizations have not been shown to be necessary–particularly at a federal level.

We know from history that injunction and conspiracy laws have often been used unfairly against political dissidents, such as labour organizers.

Moreover, the criminally violent anti-government organizations which are the focus of today's hearing are, almost without exception, tiny. Prosecution of the handful of criminal individuals involved will suffice to destroy the pathetic 'organization' itself.

New federal mandatory minimums seem, sadly, to be instinctive reaction of some persons to almost every human ill. Mandatory minimums, by their nature, prevent judges and prosecutors from tailoring the punishment to the facts of the particular case, and as a result, injustice too often results. Some of the new proposed mandatory minimums for 'violent anti-government extremists' would impose a two-year mandatory minimum on someone who shoved a policeman during an argument over a traffic ticket, a two-year mandatory minimum on a jilted teenage girl who sent her rival an anonymous letter 'I'm going to tear your eyes out,' and an eight year mandatory minimum on a homeowner who waved a baseball bat at a zoning inspector. None of these activities are justified, of course, and none of them are the intended target of the proposed mandatory minimums. But mandatory minimums are perversely designed to apply remedies which seem appropriate in the abstract to situations where they may be wildly inappropriate.

Oddly, today's hearings about 'Violent Anti-government Groups' and the threat they pose to local governments may be used to promote legislation aimed squarely at constricting, not helping, local governments. According to Section 7 of the draft 'Republican Form of Government Guarantee Act,' when county governments enforce state and local laws against what they believe to be illegal conduct by federal employees, the federal government will become the judge of its own case. Rather than having the dispute settled by a neutral arbiter–the courts–the dispute will be investigated by the federal employees own chief lawyer (the Attorney General), who may then unilaterally withhold Payments in Lieu of Taxes from the county.

It is an elementary principle of justice that no person (nor the person's attorney) can be the judge of his own case. And it's a misuse of language to claim that the federal executive's judging its own case in disputes with counties will somehow further the federal government's obligation to guarantee to each state a republican form of government. County commissioners are, after all, democratically elected. They-not the federal executive branch–are part of a state's republican form of government. Equating all militias with white supremacists is nonsense. Like the Los Angeles Police Department, some militias may have members, or even officers, who are racist, but that does not mean that the organization as a whole, or the vast majority of its members are racists. Most militias are composed of people with jobs and families; people who are seeking to protect what they have, not to inflict revenge on others for their own failings.

The frenzy of hatred being whipped up against law-abiding militia members is not unlike the hatred to which law-abiding Arab-Americans would have been subjected, had Oklahoma City been perpetrated by the Libyan Secret Service. It is not unlike the hatred to which Japanese-Americans were subjected after World War II. Ironically, some politicians who complain about the coarse, angry tone of American politics do so in speeches in which they heap hate-filled invective upon anyone and everyone who belongs to a militia.

We must remember that it is lawful in the United States to exercise freedom of speech and the right to bear arms. Spending one's weekends in the woods practicing with firearms and listening to right-wing political speeches is not my idea of a good time, but there is not, and should not, be anything illegal about it.

If we want to shrink the militia movement, the surest way is to reduce criminal and abusive behaviour by the federal government, and to require a thorough, open investigation by a Special Prosecutor of what happened at Waco and at Ruby Ridge, Idaho. If, as the evidence strongly suggests, the law was broken, the law-breakers should be prosecuted, even if they happen to be government employees.

Conversely, the persons responsible for the deaths of innocent Americans should not be promoted to even-higher positions in the FBI or federal law enforcement. If the Clinton administration were trying to fan the flames of paranoia, it could hardly do better than to have appointed Larry Potts second-in-command at the FBI.

Militias and patriot groups have been understandably ridiculed for a paranoid world-view centred on the United Nations and international banking. But ironically, many of the people doing the ridiculing share an equally paranoid world-view. Some members of the media and the gun control movement have no more idea what a real militia member is like than militia members have about what a real international banker is like. In both cases, stereotyping substitutes for understanding, and familiar devils (the United Nations for the militia, the National Rifle Association for the establishment media) are claimed to be the motive force behind the actions of a man who (allegedly) believes that the government put a microchip in his buttocks.

Morris Dees of the Southern Poverty Law Centre has begun promoting a federal ban on group firearms training which is not authorized by state law. First of all, state governments are perfectly capable of banning or authorizing whatever they want. The proposal for a federal ban amounts to asking Washington for legislation similar to that which various allies of Mr. Dees promoted at the state level in the 1980s, with little success. The majority of states having rejected a training ban, the federal government should hardly impose the will of the minority on the rest of the states.

A former direct-mail fund-raiser for the anti-gun lobby, Mr. Dees may be forgiven for a low level of concern for the exercise of the right to keep and bear arms. But the right to keep and bear arms necessarily includes the right to practice with them, just as the constitutional right to read a newspaper editorial about political events necessarily includes the right to learn how to read. Just as the government may not forbid people from learning how to read in groups, it may not forbid people from learning how to use firearms in groups.

'Government is the great teacher,' Justice Brandeis told us. Without the unjustifiable, illegal, militaristic, deadly federal violence at Ruby Ridge and at Waco, there would be no militia movement. The federal government should set a better example. If Ruby Ridge had led to a real investigation and corrective measures–instead of years of cover-up by both the Bush and Clinton administrations-then we would not be in the current situation.

The American Liberals

For American Liberals, Thomas Jefferson is the cultural hero *par excellence,* cherished for his positions on freedom of expression and on separation of Church and State and for his populistic rhetoric. (That this was a populism for whites only is a fact which American liberals have managed not to address.)

Of course, Jefferson is a hero to many Americans apart from liberals, and his admirers include, as we now know, some white right-wing terrorists. On July 3,1995, the *Washington Post* published Serge Kovaleski's profile of Terry Lynn Nichols, the second man charged in the Oklahoma City bombing. According to Kovaleski, Nichols read the works of Thomas Jefferson and Thomas Paine and was particularly inspired by Jefferson's maxim: 'The tree of liberty must be refreshed from time to time with the blood of patriots and tyrants.'

According to CNN News (January 31, 1996), the first suspect in the Oklahoma City bombing, Timothy McVeigh, was wearing a T-shirt carrying those same words at the time he was arrested while driving away from Oklahoma City. The CNN correspondent, Susan Candiotti, put a question about the T-shirt to McVeigh's lawyer, Stephen Jones. Jones replied: 'Well, if Thomas Jefferson said it, I don't think it would be incriminating at all.'

Jefferson did say it. He wrote those words in a letter to William Stevens Smith on November 13, 1787. Jefferson was writing from Paris, where he was Minister Plenipotentiary at the time, but the words do not imply any premonition of impending revolution in France. They are used in justification of Shays' Rebellion in Massachusetts. In the letter to Smith, the words, 'It is its natural manure,' appear after 'blood of partriots and tyrants.'

Jefferson did not have the French Revolution in mind when he wrote those words. But as soon as that Revolution began he wrote about it in the 'tree of liberty' spirit, and set virtually no limits to the amount of blood the French Revolutionaries might legitimately shed in the cause of liberty–'Rather than it should have failed, I would have seen half the earth desolated.' So Jefferson wrote in January 1793 after the news of the September massacres in Paris had reached America.

Liberalism and terrorism appear as opposing concepts. But they have something in common. Both belong to the large and heterogeneous family of the devotees of freedom. Freedom is the most powerful and the most ambiguous of abstract ideas. There are two main divisions within the massive ambiguities. There is freedom combined with order and limited by law. This is the freedom of England's Glorious Revolution and of the American Constitution. This is the 'manly, moral, regulated liberty' which Burke defended in *Reflections on the Revolution in France*. This is the freedom of the mainstream liberal tradition in the English-speaking world. And it is also the freedom of the mainstream *conservative* tradition in the same world. In their philosophy of freedom, the common ground between the two traditions is more important than the differences. Edmund Burke belongs to both those traditions, and no one should seek to wrest him for one of them in order to monopolize him for the other.

Much of the world today breathes what Edmund Burke called 'the wild *gas*' of liberty. Burke used that phrase about the French Revolution in the condition it was in 1790, a year after the fall of the Bastille, and two years before the advent of the Terror. The Whigs–the ancestors of modern liberals–believed that the French Revolution was over, having brought about the triumph of liberty. Burke was about to break with the Whigs, over that proposition.

At the level of logic, the liberal mind is in the grip of a fallacy: that terrorism can be rooted out by concessions and compromise, without any need to resort to inconvenient and painful emergency measures, like internment. This is a fallacy, because the terrorist mind is absolutist and unappeasable. Irish terrorists want to destroy Northern Ireland, and will not voluntarily stop anywhere short of that. Arab terrorists want to destroy Israel, and will not voluntarily stop anywhere short of that. Both sets of terrorists are interested in concessions and efforts at compromise only as evidence that the bombings are moving the enemy in the right direction, however slowly.

Compromises are possible, of course, but only with terrorists who are willing to become ex-terrorists, like Michael Collins in the 1920s or Arafat now. But terrorism survived the compromises. In the current case, Israel surrendered territory to Arafat, hoping to get peace in exchange.

If the terrorist threat increases in America, American Liberals are likely to oppose any counter-measures which may be proposed against it. In doing so they will claim the sanction of Thomas Jefferson, whose protests against the Alien and Sedition Acts of 1798 are part of the Charter of American Liberalism.

6

Terrorism in Assam

Insurgency in Assam

Insurgency in Assam makes for a rather complex phenomenon. The insurgents can claim a nearly one century old history of politics of parochialism in the state. Yet the fact remains that there was never a serious movement involving the masses with some emotional fervour. It was only a section of the elite classes which first created and then sought to propagate the centrifugal thoughts under various pretexts. Assam does not naturally qualify for an insurgent situation in the state as there was neither anything contentious in its creation nor is it one of the backwaters of the country. Moreover, the state has had a long history of very strong religio-cultural ties with the rest of the nation, besides some fairly rich and respectable contributions of its own to the glorious heritage of India. It can be safely argued that fissiparous aspirations were never an integral part of the *idee recue* of the people at large. Yet those elite people fanned the embers with such dexterity and manipulated it so subtly that they not only succeeded in imparting to it the colour of a blazing agitation but also ultimately grabbed political power through it. It presents a rather amusing study in paradoxes to find regular constitutional power vested in the hands of those people whose former, but now estranged, comrades-in-arms are now found *pari passu* spearheading one of the most dreaded insurgent movements of the country. The United Liberation Front of Assam (ULFA) has emerged as one of the major insurgent outfits of the region, suspected of having very strong links with the ISI as well as other important outfits of the neighbouring states like the National Socialist Council of Nagaland (NSCN). The ULFA, the NSCN and other outfits in the state have been able to maintain a fairly high degree of violence there and, despite some reverses, have been able to retain their capacity to strike their targets at will. On the other hand, as if to complete their record of failures elsewhere in the country, the security forces have not been able to produce the desired degree of success in Assam also.

In our considered opinion the Assamese elite classes really suffered from a linguo-cultural identity crisis. Since this, by itself, was not enough to garner much sympathy of the people, they sought to create the fear psychosis of relative deprivation. A man is likely to react more quickly and more violently if he is made to believe that he is not getting his 'legitimate share' and his very livelihood is endangered. A convenient bugbear was also readily available in the form of the so-called immigrants from other states. While it is true that the British had been bringing some educated Bengalis to work as their clerical staff; some Marwaris had come in to fill the necessities of trade and business created by economic development under the British rule; some people from East Bengal had come in to settle as agriculturists; and that labourers were brought from Bihar, U.P., Orissa and Tamil Nadu to work in the tea gardens and elsewhere, there was never any systematic and scientific study to bring forth any convincing evidence that this was causing an unjust and unfair 'relative deprivation' in respect of the Assamese lower classes. It was very easy to raise the popular allegation that the non-Assamese had come to control the economy of the state, as if it were a crime to indulge in trade and commerce anywhere in the Empire (or later in independent India). The moral, legal as well as factual hollowness of the allegation was never put to test. Then it was equally convenient to allege that the non-Assamese were not re-investing their earnings in the state, but were sending it back home. All such allegations were merely notions; the real and total impact of the immigrants on the economy of the locals was never scientifically studied, even for some purely academic interest. Once the catchwords and slogans were lobbed into the air, some people caught on to them. Even if some such study were to be undertaken, there would have been no moral or legal ground to take any action on that.

No agitator could ever produce any data on the alleged drain of wealth or attribute it to any illegal practice. No agitator could ever convince that so many Assamese lost their jobs because the outsiders took them. The employers had every right to select the cheapest and the best labourers. If the employers preferred the Bihari labourers, how could the Assamese blame the Biharis? Either the Assamese were not as efficient or they were not prepared to accept the wages offered. One could not blame the outsiders for managing to survive on the wages offered.

Separatists in Assam

A number of organisations were formed to give expression to the separatist urges of the elite classes. These included the Assam Association (1903), Asom Sahitya Sabha (1917), Asom Chhatra Sanmilan (1919), Assam Samgrakshini Sabha (1926), etc. The last one was later transformed into the Asom Jatiya Mahasabha. A notable writer and poet like Ambikagiri Roychoudhury spoke of 'Asomiya swaraj' and stated that 'swaraj for India might not bring swaraj for Assam.' The Samgrakshini Sabha demanded 'Assam for the Assamese.' These elite classes were quite apprehensive of the provincial government dominated by the Muslim League accusing it of encouraging Muslim immigration from East Bengal. Their misgivings were increased further when Bengali was introduced as the official language of the province in 1937. The Jatiya Mahasabha submitted a memorandum to the British Parliamentary Delegation on January 29, 1946 in which, *inter alia,* it was stated that 'Assam for the Assamese is the battle-cry of all the true sons of Assam.' A few months later they submitted a memorandum to the AICC also in which they threatened that they were even prepared to 'plunge the country in desperate struggle' for their 'emancipation' and 'existence.'

After independence also, it was asserted in a meeting of the Jatiya Mahasabha, Kamrup Branch, that 'Assam should come out of the Indian Union and become an independent country.' Such sentiments which were supported before independence by members of the Assamese intelligentsia like Jnannath Bora and Nilmoni

Phukann, continued to get the support of others of their ilk after independence also. G.S. Bhattacharya declared: "As to plea of Assam proper being too small for statehood, it may be observed that both in point of view of population and resources, Assam is in a much better position than any sovereign state in Europe or America. Some others went further and tried to deny Assam's religio-cultural ties with India *ab initio.* S.K. Baruah stated: "Culturally, racially and linguistically, every non-Assamese is a foreigner in Assam. In this connection we must bear in mind that Assam, from the very ancient times, never formed a part of India. Mythology and legendary allusions apart, viewed in this perspective, every foreigner who came to and resided in Assam for trade and other purposes after the occupation of the province by the British in 1826 A.D. might be treated as alien (sic)."

As the years passed, the Centre's inability to deal with the situation firmly enabled the separatist sentiments to graduate from the Language Movement (1960) to the Oil Refinery Movement (1967); and from the movement on the issue of the medium of instruction (1972) to the Anti-Foreigner Movement (1979–85). It was during the murky days of the Anti-Foreigner Movement that the ULFA came into being. A terrorist organisation by the name of Assam People's Liberation Army (APLA) was also formed about the same time by one Arpan Bezbaruah at Tezpur. They did commit a number of terrorist acts including the killing of police officers before the Assam State Assembly election in 1983: However, gradually they faded out of existence because of their own weaknesses and many of their members joined the ULFA.

The Activity of ULFA

The ULFA leaders were members of the All Assam Students Union (AASU) during the Assam agitation. After the Assam Gana Parishad (AGP) came to power, most of the AASU leaders went on to form the Government. However, there were some who did not do so. They gathered together and under the leadership of one Paresh Barua of Chabua, district Dibrugarh, re-activated the ULFA.

It may afford some interest to readers to note that the ULFA had established contact with the National Socialist Council of Nagaland (NSCN) in 1981 itself for procuring arms and arranging for training. It is learnt that by July 1983 they had started crossing over to Myanmar for training. The cadres were sent across the international border via Nagaland and Arunachal Pradesh. Now they are learnt to have established their own training camps in the foothill areas of Bhutan, Arunachal Pradesh and Nagaland bordering Assam. The ULFA has also established contact with the Kachin Independent Army (KIA) of Myanmar and through them they have been able to procure arms and other assistance from China also. The ULFA is also in touch with the People's Liberation Army (PLA) and People's Revolutionary Army of Langleipak in Manipur. It is suspected that they have plans to establish their bases in Bangladesh also with the help of the Meitei insurgents located in Bangladesh.

The general objective of ULFA can be mentioned as follows:

1. To obtain Assam's sovereignty by armed revolution.
2. To safeguard the people and interests of Assam and those of its neighbouring land, that is, Nagaland, Manipur, Mizoram, Meghalaya, Arunachal Pradesh and Tripura.
3. To have full control over the revenue resources of Assam like oil and natural gas, forests, etc.
4. To gain public support against Indian and non-Indian exploitation.
5. To stand against any suppression and repression of the Assamese masses.

The ULFA unleashed its reign of terror in earnest in 1989. There were selective killings of non-Assamese, particularly those who had substantial business interests in Assam. This included people who had settled in Assam for several generations. Then they went on a systematic spree of extortion. There has hardly been any business family in the state which has not received threatening letters for money. There have been kidnappings galore for ransom.

Over the years the nefarious activities of the ULFA have been continuing virtually unchecked. Some sincere police officers allege that undue leniency has been shown by the judiciary in dealing with the terrorists. It has also been alleged that there had been pressure of the AASU on the AGP government for not taking stern action against the ULFA. The army has been equally unsuccessful. The much publicised 'Operation Bajrang' was launched towards the close of 1990. It ended in a colossal failure. No hard core ULFA insurgent was killed or captured. Apparently they managed to flee to the neighbouring states of Arunachal Pradesh, Nagaland,

Manipur, Mizoram and Meghalaya. Short-sighted as the administration happens to be, no attempt was made to track them down there. There were no recoveries of any sophisticated arms. All that the army could find at the deserted ULFA camps was some dilapidated rifles, empty shelters and a mass grave. It has been alleged that the scheduled date and time of the imposition of President's Rule was published in a Calcutta newspaper and in a Guwahati newspaper two days before the actual event, thus providing enough warning to the ULFA leaders to vanish.

The Bodos

Bodos are the tribals of the plains. They include the Bodos, the Boro-Kacharis and the Mechas besides eight other small tribes. They are found mainly in the district of Kokrajhar and in the Udalguri sub-division of Darrang district. In all 23 development blocks in the districts of Kokrajhar, Bongaigaon, Barpeta, Nalbari, Kamrup and Darrang have been identified having a sizeable concentration of the tribals.

The Bodos have been demanding a separate state for themselves within the framework of the Constitution. The proposed state comprises the area between Arunachal Pradesh and Bhutan north of the river Brahmaputra, besides an autonomous area for the Rabhas and the Tiwas on the southern side of the river Brahmaputra. Further, they demand that Bodo language should be included in the Eighth Schedule of the Constitution and that it be made an associate official language in all the districts of Assam.

As such the demand for Bodoland should not be a matter of serious concern for the nation state, as it could be deliberated upon in due course. However, the path of terrorism which they have adopted to force their demands is a matter of concern.

Apparently the Bodos were inspired by the hill tribes, namely, Khasis, Garos, Jaintias, Mizos and Nagas agitating for separation from Assam and securing separate states in the Sixties. They also formed a Plains Tribal Council of Assam (PTCA) in 1967 for a separate Bodoland to be called 'Udayachal' with a Union Territory status. Their students' wing was known as the All Bodo Students Union (ABSU). Due to personality clashes, intra-party rivalries and differences over minor issues, these organisations split and re-split into a number of outfits. The urge for a separate state received a fresh impetus by the example of the triumphant Gorkha National Liberation Front (GNLF) movement. In fact the Bodo terrorist activities assumed serious dimensions after 1989. They included various acts of sabotage of government property, attacks on police and market places, etc.

It was rather disappointing to note that the acts of terrorism had continued even when the Bodos were taking part in negotiations with the Government. Still an agreement could be arrived at on February 20, 1993. This is known as the Bodo Accord. Among other things, it envisaged the constitution of a Bodo Autonomous Council (BAC). The BAC was to have, besides the Bodo representatives, a certain number of seats reserved for the non-Bodos residing in the area. It was to have 40 elected members and an Executive Body to carry out the functions assigned by the BAC Act to be passed later by the Assam Legislative Assembly. The BAC was supposed to exercise autonomy in matters like agriculture, small scale and cottage industries, education and irrigation, etc. Above all, the terrorists were supposed to lay down their arms and surrender.

Unfortunately, the expected did not happen. While some terrorists led by Premsing Brahma did surrender, many of them refused to do so. These fugitives are still carrying out terrorist activities. All sorts of splinter groups emerged in the process. Now the so-called Bodo Liberation Tigers (BLT) continues to press for a full-fledged state whereas the National Democratic Front of Boroland (NDFB) has edged forward to demand a separate sovereign country altogether!

The Bodo problem, in its magnitude, is not as vexatious as other problems in the region are. However, it is an affront to the might of the nation that even such a small band could not be rendered *hors de combat* so far. Odd, we should say–very odd! But this only proves that there is something fundamentally wrong in our entire approach to counterinsurgency or anti-terrorism. If we cannot contain the depredations of such small groups, how can we ever expect to be able to cope with foreign-supported large groups?

Insurgent Groups in Assam

Presently, besides the ULFA and NSCN (I/M) and NSCN (K), the other insurgent/terrorist groups active in the state include the NDFB, the BLT and the Dimasa Halam Daogha (DHD).

It impresses one with a most depressing feeling to acknowledge the fact that the violence perpetrated by these groups rose steadily from 1992 till 1998, when it reached a new peak. A marginal decline was noted in 1999.

There were a total of 735 incidents of insurgent/terrorist violence in the state in 1998. In these incidents 603 persons, including 72 security forces personnel were killed. In the year 1999 till September 30, there were 330 incidents in which 228 persons were killed. However, as we stated above, no great significance ought to be attached to figures alone. For example, in 1999, till September 30, the number of security forces personnel killed had gone up from 45 in the corresponding period of 1998 to 60 in 1999. Similarly, we maintain that readers should be cautioned about reading too much into journalistic statements like the claim that while the violence by the ULFA, the NSCN, the NDFB, and the BLT was declining, the violence by the DHD was increasing. To get bogged down in such micro details is to miss the macro picture. Policy makers and senior officers should realise that at their level a keen perception of the overall picture is vital. Transient variations in insurgent violence, unless they point to a very definite trend and are supported by other corroborative evidence, are of no great consequence. Only those who do not have the intellectual capacity to visualise the *tout ensemble* attempt to bluff their way through half-baked statistics. At the *policy making level* one should get to the bottom of the matter. In the context of insurgent violence in Assam, the *fin mot,* the essence of the situation is that the ability of the insurgents to cross the border; their arms holding; their training facilities; their hard core leaders; their foreign connections with the ISI, the KIA and China; and above all their capacity to strike their targets almost at will remains by and large intact.

It is important to note that while practically the whole of Assam has been affected by insurgent violence, the situation is worse in the districts of Kokrajhar, Barpeta, Nalbari, Kamrup and Darrang. These five districts account for 47 per cent of the total violence in the state. The situation is pretty bad in the hill districts of N.C. Hills and Karbi Anglong also.

An interesting feature of insurgency in Assam is the audacity of the ULFA in almost flaunting its ISI links. It should be worthwhile to recall that during the Kargil conflict, the ULFA had not hesitated a bit in adopting a blatantly pro-Pak stand. This is an extremely serious matter. We are saying so because in most of the cases the bugaboo of the so-called 'ISI involvement' is raised by the intelligence agencies in a shameful attempt to cover up their own incompetence. There is no reason at all to even suspect that the ISI could be as omnipotent, as omniscient and as omnipresent as it is popularly made out to be. When the officials in general and the intelligence agencies in particular harp on the ubiquitous involvement of the ISI, their real intention is always to conceal the fact that they are simply not able to first comprehend and then to be in command of a purely internal problem. It is so very easy to fool the public all the time by invoking the 'foreign hand.' Once upon a time it used to be the CIA; now it is the ISI. The ISI men must be laughing up their sleeves. Every time there is an explosion of a country-made bomb, intelligence agencies lose no time in declaring the ISI hand behind it. Some self-styled bomb expert who cannot distinguish plastic explosive from ordinary soap, would make a pompous visit to the scene of explosion, cast a cursory glance at the damage and announce that RDX was used in the explosion! Then the politicians can also join to accuse the ISI of trying to de-stabilise this country by vitiating the communal atmosphere and so forth.

It is really infinitely interesting to find the silliness some match by the hypocrisy of others. The people and the government agencies are really made for each other. God bless the invisible 'foreign hand'! But for the 'foreign hand,' there would be hardly anything which the politicians might use for throwing the blame on. But for the 'foreign hand,' the government agencies would not be able to perpetuate and justify their own comfortable existence–neither would the behemoth of the army be able to spend billions of rupees on the creature comforts of its officers nor would the intelligence agencies be able to claim and siphon off untold loads of money in the garb of the alleged secret service funds. In the context of the ULFA it is, therefore, imperative that the ISI connection be taken serious note of. A country which is lulled into languidness as everybody takes to crying wolf too often, would be in for a really nasty surprise when the wolf really appears. It makes eminent strategic sense for Pakistan to instigate insurgency in the North-Eastern states also. If they have been able to do that, they must be given credit for overcoming the handicap of race, religion and culture in the furtherance of their sinister designs. This master stroke on their part demands the utmost sincerity and an equally skilful application on our part to counter it.

Another disturbing trend in Assam is the build up of ethnic tension as the NDFB continues to target the non-Bodos (the Santhals in particular) as a part of its 'ethnic cleansing programme.' The BLT, at least for the time being, is showing some signs of complaisance. However, that should not divert our attention from the fact that about 1 per cent of the population of the state has been forced to survive in refugee camps in the Kokrajhar district in the most miserable conditions. That in itself has the potential of maintaining the animosity at a high level.

7

Insurgency in Nagaland

History of the Naga People

For the purpose of this treatise it is not necessary to trace the origin of the Naga people. Thus it is immaterial to discuss whether they are indigenous to this land or had migrated to this place from further East. We do not consider it honourable to stake a claim to national integration by citing some passage in the Mahabharata which could be alluded to contain some proof of the old ties of the Nagas with the rest of the country. It does not augur well for a nation if it is obliged to seek national integration through such contrived means.

Our research findings concur with those who maintain that there is no reference to the Nagas in the chronicles of the early Hindu kings of Kamrupa during the period of fourth to thirteenth centuries. However, some references are found in the Buranjis, the chronicles of the Ahom kings of Assam beginning in the thirteenth century.

In the subsequent period we find that the Nagas, in their dealings with the Ahoms, were quite like the North-West Frontier tribes who had vexed and taxed the patience of the Mughals. The Nagas too resorted to frequent raids upon the villages in the plains, the basic objective being plunder. The Ahom rulers lacked the muscle to contain them. Apparently they did not suffer from any ego problems in admitting their military incompetence and sought to buy peace rather than maintain it. Thus appeasement became the guiding principle of their policy towards the Nagas. It manifested itself in various forms. With tribes like Lotha, Konyak and Ao, the 'Posa' system meant payment by the plainspeople to satisfy the depredators. With the Nagas of the Patkoi range the 'Khat' system meant the allotment of some land in the foothills. We maintain that this policy of appeasement, like similar policies anywhere else in the world, helped only in making the tribals more belligerent. There is no reason to describe it as some authors do, as a tactful or successful policy. Good governance is not synonymous with such trade offs.

The British had their first armed encounter with the Nagas in the course of the construction of a road connecting Assam and Manipur. Suitable punitive measures were undertaken and in 1850 the British went on to capture a Naga fort also at Konemah. The junior officers in the field were naturally inclined towards a complete military subjugation. However, the higher formations vacillated. Dalhousie himself observed: "I dissent entirely from the policy which is recommended of what is called obtaining a control, that is to say, of taking possession of those hills and of establishing our sovereignty over their savage inhabitants. Our possession could bring no profit to us and would be as costly to us as it would be unproductive." Even in 1873, the Lt. Governor, George Campbell was of the opinion that they could manage-to establish political control and influence over the tribes without any overt assertion of actual sovereignty over the tribal areas! Gradually, however, the proponents of a more active policy started gaining the upper hand. In order to ensure some administrative control, the Naga Hills were first declared a 'Scheduled District' and later a 'Backward Tract' of Assam. A Political Agent was installed in Kohima in 1879. Still the administration did not really go beyond occasional interference in the cases of inter-tribal or inter-village clashes or in the cases of depredatory raids by the Nagas upon the plainsmen. Indifference, vagueness and the lack of a firm resolve continued to characterise the British administration even during the opening decades of the twentieth century. The British did not mind the creation of an organisation called the Naga Club either by those Nagas who harboured the dreams of independent Naga Hills. This Naga Club even submitted a memorandum to the Simon Commission. Eventually the Government of India Act, 1935, admitted the Naga Hills as 'Excluded Area' that is, excluded from the normal provincial administration.

The British had no single good reason to be deeply interested in the Nagas. Their concern diminished even more when the ominous clouds of the Second World War engulfed the Empire. This emboldened the Nagas further. They knew it well that the British were too strong for them. Hence, they could not afford a rebellion against them.

The Nagas' streak of insubordination and their indifference to the Indian consciousness was very much evident in the memorandum they submitted to J.P. Mills, Adviser to the Governor for Tribal Affairs in 1945: "We the Nagas are not ready to take our place in a democratic constitution or to compete with the sophisticated so called Indian politicians. We the Nagas became dependent only on the British. It is immaterial to us who rules Hindustan or Pakistan as long as we are the subjects of the British, under the Great King of Britain."

Z.A. Phizo, who was later to become the leader of the insurgents, had crossed over to Burma in 1942 itself with his band of followers. He himself admitted that he was in touch with the Japanese who, no doubt, filled his dreams of an independent state with vivid colours. The Naga National Council (NNC) was formed in 1946. Initially they demanded only local autonomy within Assam administration. Perhaps a realisation was sinking in that after all India was not going to be as weak as they had expected it to be. This made the Nagas decidedly nervous and rash as time was rapidly slipping out. In February 1947 they said that they would be prepared to accept the sovereignty of India after its independence for a period of ten years, after which they should have the right of self-determination. Three months later they sent a delegation to meet the Governor of Assam. In July they approached Mahatma Gandhi with their demand of independence. A decision was, in any case, not expected and Phizo lost no time in declaring the independence of the Naga Hills on August 14, 1947 itself. He was arrested in 1951 but released shortly thereafter. That marked the beginning of the unfortunate soft-pedalling which allowed the problem to assume its present proportions. A soon as Phizo was out of jail, he became the president of the NNC and advanced the claim that he had held a plebiscite in which 99 per cent of the Nagas had voted for independence!

Naga Insurgency

If just one word were to be chosen to describe the phenomenon of insurgency in Nagaland, it would be tenacity. If just one word were to be chosen to portray the way we have handled the situation so far, it would be incompetence. The first incident of insurgency in Nagaland was reported way back in 1955. Forty-five long years have passed since the first report of the Ministry of Defence in which attention was drawn to the hostile activities of the Nagas causing a deterioration in the public order situation in the NEFA. It may afford us with considerable interest to note that though the public order situation was stabilised somewhat with the help of the army, the disturbances spread to the Naga Hills and there they could not be controlled even by the army. Forty-five years later sulky defiance has changed into an open defiance. 'The National Socialist Council of Nagaland (NSCN) is not only stronger than ever, it has been found rendering quite active assistance to the insurgent groups of other states as well. The insurgents have been allowed to graduate from their primitive spears to modern machine guns. The security forces, the intelligence machinery and the administration are all involved more than ever in the counterinsurgency efforts, but still where are we? We are inclined to believe, and *a fortiori*, that this provides an excellent illustration of the tragic incompetence of all concerned. The security forces have not been able to adapt themselves to the complexities of jungle warfare or improvise, not to speak of mastering them. The intelligence machinery has remained a massive assemblage of farces of astronomical proportions. As for the politicians, they have excelled in nothing but dramatics–pompous statements accompanied by some not very droll dancing with the tribals, as if the roots of the problem lay in the nation not having been able to properly appreciate their traditional dress and headgear all these years. Admittedly, a *demarche* has never been the *forte* of the politicians of this nation; they could be pardoned for that, but still there is every reason to demand a more sincere, earnest and scientific approach.

Naga insurgency presents some singularly novel features of its own. It is most illuminating to note that it has, on an ideological level, hardly anything of substance in it. And yet it has managed to survive for so long. The romantics of a 'red revolution' must learn a lesson from this. Crudity does have an intrinsic appeal; it is all the more attractive for a primitive mindset. One can take out facts in isolation, distort history at will, draw utterly simplistic inferences, and still be able to get a remarkably large number of people who would eagerly lap it up.

In the early years of insurgency, before he managed to escape first to Dacca in December 1959 and eventually to England, Phizo had directed the movement with utmost care. It was a copybook example with elaborate political and armed wings–the political wing carrying out extensive agitprop among the people (especially through key persons like the village elders), recruiting supporters, raising funds through taxes, and suitably guiding the armed wing. Phizo also set up separate youth and women wings of the movement. In effect, the political wing was able to run an almost parallel government in its areas of influence. That was quite a remarkable achievement considering the fact that the number of armed insurgents hardly ever exceeded the figure of 3,000.

Much of the credit of the military aspect of the insurgency goes to redoubtable leaders like Kaito Sema and Mowu Angami. The operational part of the core of the movement was structured so meticulously that in spite of the flight of Phizo, the movement could maintain its momentum till 1964. Cracks began to appear after that.

Phizo's flight had a catastrophic effect on the movement. As the emotional fervour subsided in due course of time, there were to be found many leaders who gave vent to their suppressed desire of a negotiated settlement. The Naga People's Convention, formed in 1957, was instrumental in securing statehood for Nagaland in 1963. Then a political party known as the Naga Nationalist Organisation was formed. It took part in the election and formed the first government of the new state. It may be recalled that Phizo's policy of intolerance to any opposition had made the movement lose many sincere leaders. Gradually inter-tribal rivalries and feuds came to the fore. In the absence of a strong cohesive force which could have been provided by a solid ideological basis, these rivalries started sapping the movement of its vitality. It should be instructive to note that there are at least 14 distinct tribes among the Nagas. It had so happened that most of the military leaders came from the Sema tribe whereas most of the political leaders, including Phizo himself, came from the Angami tribe.

The Burmese authorities arrested Phizo in 1952 when he crossed over to Burma. He was handed over to the Indian authorities. Once again he was released after a short period. It would do some good to the readers to compare the treatment in respect of Phizo with that in respect of Sheikh Abdullah in Kashmir. It should be quite apparent that the capacity to procrastinate and delude oneself at the same time knows no bounds. Thenceforth Phizo was to remain cautious and avoid arrest. The movement became an underground one and Phizo continued to sow the seeds of insurrection among the tribals through his extensive tours.

As expected, the supporters of Phizo, hiding in Myanmar, repudiated the Shillong Accord. This Accord also led to the birth of another organisation called the National Socialist Council of Nagaland (NSCN). It was formed by a Naga, Th. Muivah and a man called Isak Chish Swu from the Tangkhul tribe of Myanmar. They lost no time in repudiating the Accord and dubbing the NNC leaders who had signed the Accord as 'traitors.' The movement is now being spearheaded by the NSCN, and the Naga Federal Government (NGF) of the Phizo supporters occupies a secondary position.

At an ideological level, the NSCN provides a curious rehash of several ideologies. While speaking of socialism, the NSCN manifesto states that: "We stand for socialism because it is the only social and economic system that does away with exploitation and ensures fair equality to all the people." In its opinion, socialism must ensure 'freedom from the fear of economic exploitation and political domination and suppression.' Yet it disapproves of both the Chinese and the Soviet varieties of socialism and describes its own as the Naga variety of socialism owing allegiance to the Christian faith. Apparently they are aware that most of the Nagas are Christians and that it would not be advisable to overlook it. They are also aware that the NNC leaders who had signed the Accord, had denounced them as 'communists' so that they could be branded anti-Christian. Furthermore, with the given state of inter-tribal differences, Christianity is arguably a very important unifying factor. The NSCN, therefore, provides for a Ministry of Religious Affairs and a separate council called the 'Council of Nagaland Churches' also.

Naga Insurgent Groups

At present three major insurgent groups are active in Nagaland. Since 1988 the NSCN has split into two groups on account of some ideological different and inter-tribal feuds. One group owes allegiance to Isak and Muivah. It is known as NSCN (I/M). The other group IS led by one S.S. Khaplang of Myanmar. It is known as NSCN (K). The dissident group of the Naga National Council which had formed the Naga Federal Government is known as NNC (A)/NFG. It is believed that there are friendly relations between the NSCN (K) and NNC (A)/NFG.

All the three outfits have got their headquarters in Myanmar territory across the Manipur border. Most of their bases and training camps are located in the Chittagong Hills of Bangladesh and Arakan and Somra Hills of Myanmar. They have now developed such close relations with China that they not only procure arms and ammunition for themselves but also escort insurgents of outfits belonging to other states to China for similar assistance. They also have very friendly relations with the Karen and Kachin Insurgents of Myanmar. Besides China, some arms are learnt to be obtained from the arms market in Thailand also.

The NSCN (I/M) is the most dominant insurgent group in the state. Its areas of influence in the state include Dimapur, Zunheboto, Wokha and parts of Mokokchung, Kohima, and Tuensang districts besides the Ukhrul district of Manipur and Tirup district in Arunachal Pradesh. The NSCN (K) has got considerable influence in Mon and parts of Tuensang, Mokokchung and Kohima districts. The NNC (A)/NFG is active in parts of Phek and Tuensang districts.

There are definite Indications that the NSCN groups are having links with the ULFA and the Boro Security Force. As a result, they have been able to extend their activities into the North Cachar Hills, forest reserves of Karbi Anglong district, and the tea-gardens along the Assam-Nagaland border.

In outrageous affront to the nation, the insurgent groups have been consistently able to indulge in terrorist activities with a considerable degree of impurity. These include attacks on government forces and various act of sabotage of public property. While such activities could be tolerated to some extent as an integral and unavoidable part of any violent movement, a more disgraceful part is the fact that they are still able to run a parallel government in several parts of the state. Still 'taxes' are collected by them. Still people regard them as almost invincible in their areas of influence. Still the forces find themselves as helpless and confused as they used to be forty-five years ago.

It should humour the readers to note that this insolent mockery of the might of the nation is sought to be explained by some singularly novel theories. The first is that the insurgents have got very sophisticated weapons. We have blasted this shameful theory elsewhere in this book. The Nagas started the insurgency with their primitive spears and a few muzzle-loaders. If they have been able to raise their standard to AK rifles, whose fault is this? And what is sophisticated weaponry? Are we fighting with the medieval Bandooq Toradars? Are we not having much more sophisticated weaponry? Or are we able to fight only those adversaries who have got much inferior weapons? So much for the *enfant gate* we have! The second is that the insurgents operate from very remote and inaccessible areas. That is quite amusing. If a terrain is difficult for our soldiers, it is difficult for the insurgents also. Do we expect that the enemy will oblige us by fighting on a ground of our choice? A similarly puerile excuse was heard during the Kargil conflict also. Admittedly, the terrain was pretty rough and the climate rather inhospitable. But it was so for the intruders also. If they could fight there, what was so arduous for our soldiers? Then they said that our soldiers were not properly equipped to fight in that place at that height. Well, the audacity of those who put forward such theories must be admired, the gullibility of those who lap it up must be deprecated.

Presently, the insurgents are indulging in a large number of extortion cases, particularly in the urban centres including Kohima and Dimapur. These activities are going on unchecked. It presents an illuminating example of the fear in the minds of the people and the inability of the secruity machinery to instil any confidence in them. As we have discussed elsewhere at length in this book, countering insurgency is not the job of guns alone. The insurgents have been able to keep a significant fraction of the non-governmental organisations (NGOs) on their side which carry out tendentious propaganda about instances of human rights violations by the security forces. They do not have any scruples about distorting certain facts or about simple gross exaggeration.

The present situation in Nagaland is rather confusing. We have now a cease-fire with both the NSCN(I/M) and the NSCN(K). The cease-fire with the NSCN(I/M) is nearly four years old, whereas the cease-fire with the NSCN(K) has been announced only recently. We find that the attitude and the behaviour of the NSCN(I/M) has been somewhat intriguing even when they had formally accepted the cease-fire. It may be recalled that when election was held in the state in September 1999, the NSCN(I/M) had opposed it openly and the Naga Hoho had gone to the extent of raising the slogan of 'Solution, Not Election.' Even now we find that the NSCN(I/M) is not treating the Government of India with the respect it deserves. Some of their old fulminations have been narrated in the 'Notes' at the end of this section. Recently, they have spewed some more venom. Media reports (for example, write-up entitled 'Naga cease-fire runs into rough weather,' by the special correspondent, *The Hindu*, May 09, 2001) quote extensively from the statement of the NSCN(I/M). The NSCN(I/M) does not seem very pleased with the announcement of the cease-fire with the NSCN(K). In fact, its statement was issued shortly after the cease-fire with the NSCN(K) was announced. It described the NSCN(K) as a surrogate outfit supported by the Nagaland Government.

Consequently, it dubbed the cease-fire as a 'marriage of a mother to daughter.' Having thus ridiculed the cease-fire with the NSCN(K), the NSCN(I/M) has demanded that its own cease-fire be reviewed within two weeks. They also demanded that the matter should be treated 'seriously.' This appears to be a pressure tactic as a review of the cease-fire with the NSCN(I/M) is due only at the end of July 2001. The NSCN(I/M) stated: "As the Government has betrayed its commitments, the NSCN(I/M) has no moral obligation to respect the Government's commitments anymore." We feel that this is not the way for an insurgent outfit to treat a government. Not only that, the NSCN(I/M) charged the Government with going back on its assurances. What assurances they have been referring to is not known to us. However, the same media reports indicated that the NSCN(I/M) had made a reference to their demand of extending the cease-fire to all Naga-inhabited areas of the North-East. Details regarding this demand have been furnished in the 'Notes' at the end of this section. How is the Government going to deal with this demand is a matter of current policy and hence we cannot comment on that. The media report cited above mentioned that it was officially disclosed by the Home Ministry that discussions had been held between the Centre and the NSCN(I/M) on the extension of the ceasefire beyond Nagaland, but they had been inconclusive. Readers may appreciate the complexity of the matter by noting that this demand involves three more state governments, namely, Manipur, Assam and Arunachal Pradesh. It remains to be seen as to how they would react to this matter. There are many practical difficulties also involved in this as Assam and Manipur have got insurgency problems of their own, and the forces may not find it easy to distinguish between a Naga insurgent and those belonging to other outfits.

Some morally intriguing questions have been raised from time to time in the context of insurgency in Nagaland. Delving deep into them and attempting a thorough exposure would necessarily involve touching the so-called intelligence operations and state secrets.

8

Terrorism in Tripura, Manipur and Mizoram

The Tribal Kings of Tripura

The tribal kings of Tripura had a political as well as economic motive in rather unwittingly embarking upon a path that was to sow the seeds of rebellion. Royal recognition was sought to be achieved by placating some eminent Bengali Brahmans. This, in turn, enabled them to secure matrimonial relationships with the other established royal families in the country. So far so good, as this was their purely personal problem. However, as a measure of placation they started inviting a large number of high caste Bengalis to Tripura and provided them with plains' land for settlement. The local tribals had no knowledge of the higher modes of agricultural production and were dependent mainly on shifting cultivation (Jhum). The Bengali settlers were plough cultivators, accounting for higher production. This economic advantage, coupled with their far better educational background, enabled them to occupy a prominent place in jobs, commerce and business. The resulting social discontent needed only some excuse for a violent manifestation. The occasion came in 1939–42 when Ratan Mani, a leader of the Reang tribe, incited his people to revolt against the exorbitantly high rates of house tax imposed by the king. The natural fury of the people was excited more by their miserable condition caused by a contemporaneous drought and there were several armed encounters with the royal forces.

The dawn of independence also witnessed a massive influx of refugees from the erstwhile East Pakistan. This unnerved the tribals further. Opposing established authority was no longer a new thing, the tribals already having tasted blood in their encounters with the king's forces. A multitude of organisations sprang up in the following decade with the proclaimed effective of protecting the interests of the tribals. Their planks included opposing the repression of the tribals by the 'foreigners' with the help of the state machinery, opposing the influx of the refugees and demanding a higher participation in administration. Such organisations included the Janashiksha Samiti, the 'Seng-Krak,' the Pahari Union, the Adivasi Sangh, and the Tripura Rajya Adivasi Sangh, etc. None of these organisations could, however, make any significant impact.

The vehemence with which the TNV insurgents started their horris business took the Government by surprise. Communal tension flared up throughout the state. Systematic attacks were launched on police stations and outposts; markets were looted and public property was extensively damaged. One of the first attacks on a police station took place as early as on August 3, 1979 when the Birganj police station in south Tripura was attacked. A most real *danse macabre* was witnessed in 1980 at the massacre at Mandai near Agartala. G. Chaudhury has provided a graphic description of the situation prevailing at that time: "The flame of fire spread very rapidly from village to village burning thousands of houses and huts, cattle and crops. Numerous villages were laid waste. Lakhs of people were rendered homeless. Properties, both movable and immovable worth several crores, were destroyed, damaged, burnt, looted and captured. Hundreds were murdered. Women were raped. All contemptible crimes in human history were committed." It was obvious that there was a most reprehensible breakdown of public order in the state. The state police, the para-military forces, the army and the pretentious intelligence machinery had all failed miserably.

Almost as if paralysed by the *coup de theatre*, the administration could simply do nothing of consequence against the Devil's carnival. In form and feature, face and limb, the proceedings were ugly as sin incarnate. Ever since that period of shameful darkness, the insurgents have been following the general pattern of suddenly materialising out of the jungles, raiding a nearby habitation or government office (be it a police outpost or anything else), killing, looting, and then again vanishing into the jungles. In 1988 a tripartite agreement was signed by the Union Government, the state Government and the TNV. As usual, the agreement envisaged that the TNV would give up its secessionist policy and abjure violence. In return, the surrendered terrorists were to be rehabilitated. An important aspect of the agreement was that a constitutional amendment would be brought about to ensure that the tribals always got the number of MLAs commensurate with the proportion of their population in the state. For their satisfaction *pro tempore*, it was also promised that necessary laws would be enacted and effective action would be taken to restore the land alienated from the tribals.

At present there are as many as 12 insurgent groups active in the state. Some sources maintain that the number could be as high as 20. Two of them, namely, the NLFT and the All Tripura Tiger Force (ATTF) are the most active ones.

As anybody reading newspapers or watching television should be aware, insurgency in Tripura presents a quite grim security scenario. The violence level not only continues to be very high, it is characterised by the utmost brutality. There seems to be a strange resignation writ all over that God would not mend it, and we cannot. The state Government has declared 22 police station areas in the state as totally disturbed and five police station areas as partially disturbed under the Armed Forces (Special powers) Act. We maintain strongly and have discussed it at length elsewhere also in this book that the impact of insurgency is largely a subjective phenomenon. Figures alone cannot portray the true picture of insurgency. Yet for those readers who are very keen on statistics, it may afford them some interest to have a view of the trend of violence in the state for the past three years. In 1997 there were 303 incidents of violence in which 270 persons including 50 security forces personnel were killed. There were 568 incidents in 1998 and in which 251 persons including 25 security forces personnel lost their lives. In the first nine months of 1999 there were 455 incidents of violence in which 181 persons including 25 security forces personnel were killed; the corresponding figures for 1998 being 369 incidents and 184 casualties including 22 of the forces. In the first nine months of 1998 there were 302 kidnappings; the figure went up to 341 in 1999.

Insurgent Outfits in Tripura

Tripura is a small hilly state. It is bound by Bangladesh in the north, west and south and by Mizoram and the Chittagong Hill Tracts of Bangladesh in the east. Tripura is connected with the rest of the country through a narrow strip of land which contains the Assam-Agartala road. This road runs across four hill ranges in the state.

Nineteen different tribes have been identified in the state. Out of them the first five, in decreasing order of population, are, Tripuri, Reang, Jamatia, Chakma and Halam. It would be interesting to note that in comparison to Nagaland, Tripura suffers much less from inter-tribe rivalries. Inter-tribal rivalries account for a distinct point of weakness in the Naga movement. Conversely, a relative lack of these in Tripura could well constitute a source of strength for the movement.

Almost all the important insurgent outfits have got their bases and training camps in the Chittagong Hill Tracts. Some of them are learnt to have developed links with insurgent outfits of other states in the North-East. In fact in the days of the TNV, the Mizo National Front (MNF) used to impart training to their guerrillas. Access to Bangladesh is so easy that most of the by arms are procured through dealers and agents based in Bangladesh. Readers must ponder over the pathetic helplessness of the forces in checking this impudent arms-smuggling which has contributed greatly to the sustenance of one of the most brutal and ghoulish insurgent movements in the country.

National Liberation Front of Tripura (NLFT)

This organisation was formed in 1989 and achieved notoriety after the attack on the Tainani police outpost in 1991 in which one policeman was killed and nine rifles were looted. The first leader of the outfit was Dhananjoy Reang. Since December 1993 it is led by Biswa Mohan Deb Barma after Dhananjoy formed a different group.

The NLFT has been able to maintain a consistently high level of violence. In fact since 1988 it has emerged as one of the major insurgent groups in the entire North-East.

The NLFT has shown a very significant proclivity for extortions and kidnappings. A considerable amount of money is raised by 'taxes' extorted from all and sundry. Because of the activities of the NLFT the movement of goods and people on NH-34 and other roads has been very adversely affected; the roads are quite unsafe now. Things have come to such a pass that the areas in north Tripura and those close to Agartala in west Tripura, which were once considered relatively safer, are no longer safe at all. The *tout ensemble* of the activities of the NLFT is not limited only to the ambience of the all-pervasive feeling of insecurity, it has succeeded in re-creating that surcharged atmosphere of ethnic tension which is ominously reminiscent of the period of 1980. By selecting the victims of their violence mainly from the non-tribals (particularly the Bengalis) they have created such a strong undercurrent of ethnic tension that the slightest provocation could result in an eruption of ethnic violence. This should be able to cause not only a further deterioration in the public order situation, but also put further stress on the already stretched security apparatus.

Social Democratic Front of Tripura (SDFT)

It is believed that this group is collaborating with the NLFT. It was noticed first in January 1995. It is led by Suren Deb Barma and Sambburam Deb Barma.

Tripura Security Army (TSA)

A rather small group, it was noticed in connection with some extortion activities in January 1995.

Tripura Tribal Democratic Force (TTDF)

The original group had surrendered. Nowa splinter group led by Nayak Jamatiya survives. These were found active in Udaipur and Amarpur sub-divisions.

All Tripura Tiger Force (ATTF)

The original ATTF was known as All Tripura Tribal Force and it was deeply under the influence of the CPM. The All Tripura Tribal

Force surrendered and joined the mainstream. However, a group led by Ranjit Deb Barma did not surrender and formed the outfit known as All Tripura Tiger Force. In strength, activities and influence it is next only to the NLFT.

Tripura Resurrection Army (TRA)

This group was created by the first leader of the NLFT, Dhananjoy Reang after the split in the group. The formation of the group was announced in Bangladesh in May 1994. The area of its influence is limited to South Tripura and Dhalai districts

Tripura Tribal Youth Force (TTYF)

This outfit is led by Dartharai Tripura and Uttam Deb Barma. The members are more keen on looting and extortion.

Seng-krak

Taking after an organisation bearing the same name in the 1950s, the present organisation is led by Rajendra Reang and Samprai Deb Barma. Its activities are quite similar to those of the TTYF.

Tripura Liberation Organisation (TLO)

The important leaders of the TLO are Sampak Deb Barma, Arjun Deb Barma and Jumia Deb Barma. The organisation came to notice since January, 1994 when they were found distributing leaflets and indulging in collection of 'taxes.' In their leaflets they presented a ten-point charter of demands.

Tripura Tribal Volunteer Force (TTVF)

The important leaders of this outfit are Matindra Tripuri, Baidya Deb Barma and Bijoy Deb Barma. It has come to notice since October 1993.

All Tripura Volunteer Force (ATVF)

This outfit was noticed in September 1994. It was learnt to be led by Waishy Lal Halam and Gunanani Reang.

All Tripura Volunteer Association (ATVA)

This is an outfit which is presumably more interested in protecting the interests of the Chakma people in Supra. It is led by Kalachan Chakma and Biswanath Chakma.

Insurgency in Manipur

Insurgency in Manipur is not as much innate as it is acquired. Essentially, it is a case of infection contracted from the neighbouring states where the ambience has an insurrectionary focus. The Manipur insurgents are involved in this business because, in their perception, it is, for want of a better option, very much *de rigueur* to do so. They do not have the advantage of a history movements tinged heavily with secessionist thoughts; which some of their comrades-in-arms in other states have. In fact a communist movement in 1948 led by Hyam Irabot had floundered because the feudal loyalties of the people turned out to be much stronger than what the communists had expected. In such a backdrop it is indeed most unfortunate that the political and the economic situations in the state were consistently allowed to be manipulated in such a manner that their cumulative effect ultimately proved conducive to the growth of insurgency. Most of the insurgents are still not very clear about the exact reasons which forced them to take up arms. Some of them accuse the *ad hoc* policies of the Union Government. Some speak of the so-called sense of alienation which crept in following the failure of the political system in delivering the expected results. The armchair theorists do not tire of blaming the economic backwardness of the region and unemployment among the youth. Still others point to the rampant corruption in the body politic of Manipur, and the politician bureaucrat nexus which quietly siphoned off a large part of the Centre's largesse. Then it is also a fact that there were frequent changes of government in the 1960s and the 1970s by a multiplicity of parties at the state level driven by the most unscrupulous considerations. It should be obvious that, treated in isolation, none of these factors was potent enough to nurture insurgency. It should also be conceded that the perceived grievances of the people were not very articulate expressions of the real problems. Yet, when considered together, they seemed to exercise a synergetic effect. The combined effect of all that was going wrong in Manipur was an erosion of trust in the rulers by the people. This distrust, coupled with the exposure to insurgent movements all around and a whiff of the intoxicating communist ideology in the air, was enough to push the naturally violent natured among them over the brink.

Manipur is a predominantly hilly state. About 90 per cent of the area of the state consists of hills. The Imphal Valley has just about 10 per cent of the total area. Still, the Meitel people inhabiting the valley account about 60 per cent of the population of the state. The tribals residing in the hills contribute about 27.3 per cent of the population.

The Meities are Vaishnavite Hindus. The Lois are the scheduled caste people. They are also residents of the valley. The Bishnupunya people are concentrated in some villages around the town of Bishnupur. The Pangans are the Muslims of Manipur. They are concentrated in the area between the Imphal and the Iril rivers.

The Kukis and the Nagas have had a fairly bloody history of rivalry. There are several reasons for it. The Tangkhul Nagas are supporters of the NSCN. Thus their demand of a 'Greater Nagaland' is resented by the Kukis who regard it as a threat to their perceived integrity of Manipur. Then the Nagas and the Kukis have a serious difference of opinion on the issue of creation of a separate district for Sadar Hills with its headquarters at Kangpokpi. There have been agitations and counter-agitations on this issue by the Kukis and the Nagas leading to rather long disruptions of the lifeline of the state, namely, the Dimapur-Imphal road (NH-39). Above all, the rivalry stems from the fact that both the Kukis and the Nagas want to control the Moreh region in Chandel district. It should be kept in mind that the Moreh region is of utmost importance from the point of view of the smuggling of narcotic drugs, with its obvious impact on the health of the insurgent groups though narco-terrorism. To start with, drug smuggling was largely controlled by the NSCN. Now the Kukis have emerged as a fierce contender.

The Kuki-Naga clashes reached a peak in 1993 and are still seriously vitiating the public order climate in the state. In this connection readers may please refer to our discussion on insurgency in Nagaland also, where we have mentioned the allegation of the politicians having a hand in the continuance of the clashes.

In the absence of a coherent direction and a sound ideological basis, insurgent activities in Manipur present a fairly confusing picture of violence. We find a host of small outfits with very limited tactical objectives, and certainly neither any capability nor a design for some grand objective, fighting as vigorously against each other as they fight with the government forces. Ethnic strife is not limited to the Kukis and the Nagas only. The Paites and the Vaipheis also resent the Kukis. Partly, this could have an economic reason also. In the wake of the Kuki-Naga clashes many Kukis had migrated to the Churachandpur district. The Zomis, that is, the Paites and the

Vaipheis are apprehensive that this migration would further strain their already depleted economic resources. Although peace talks were held between the Zomi Council and the Kuki Inpi Churachandpur, a strong undercurrent of mutual mistrust still exists. The ZRA is still found to be active in the Churachandpur district.

The Meitei insurgents are quite active in the valley districts of Imphal East, Imphal West, Thoubal and Bishenpur. The usual activities of the PLA, PREPAK and the UNLF include attacks on security forces, elimination of informers and large-scale extortion. Of late a very disturbing trend has been noticed in respect of attacks on the security forces. It seems that they are more keen on attacking those units which have been inducted from outside the state. The PLA was also found distributing 'residential permits' from 1997 for the non-Manipuris. This was to serve as an immediate threat to them as a gesture of their having been got identified and also as a warning for any future action about their eventual eviction. It is also learnt that the PLA, the PREPAK, the UNLF and the KCP have come to some sort of understanding among themselves. Apparently, the idea is to form an umbrella organisation called Manipur People's Liberation Front (MPLF). If this remains on paper only then it is not a cause for any serious concern. However, if it becomes effective then we must certainly expect a substantial increase in the number of attacks on security forces.

Mizoram After Insurgency

Peace has returned to Mizoram after two decades of insurgency from 1966 to 1986. The Mizo National Front (MNF) signed the Peace Accord on June 30, 1986. Subsequently, Mizoram was raised to the status of a full-fledged state on February 20, 1987. The Accord has not been violated so far. A brief overview of the history of insurgency in Mizoram is important not only from the point of view of pure academic interest it is important because history does not really repeat itself; history teaches by analogy. The Mizoram experience should always be kept at the back of the mind for the pointers it can provide in dealing, *mutatis mufnndis,* with a similar situation elsewhere, and with some definite advantage too. There would be too many pitfalls which can be easily avoided, and at the same time, there would be many issues which would not be amenable to the placing of as much hopes in them as could be done in the case of Mizoram.

The Mizos in India comprise several different tribes, namely, Lushais, Chakmas, Pawis, Paithers, Raltese, Phangirs, Hmras, Kukis, Maras, Lakhers and Reangs. The biggest and the most advanced group among them is that of the Lushais. It may be noted that many tribes of Mizo stock are found in the neighbouring areas of Myanmar and Bangladesh also.

The British had annexed the Mizo areas in 1891. In 1898 they created the Lushai Hills district as a part of Assam. This was kept as an 'Excluded Area' like the Naga Hills. One important thing which distinguishes the behavioural pattern of the Mizos in comparison to that the Nagas, is the former's history of a relatively closer interaction with the British and the rest of the country. This could be attributed to the higher degree of advancement of the Mizo tribes, the higher spread of education, or both. The fact remains that the Mizos had served in the British army as porters even during the First World War. In the Second World War they graduated to the ranks of fighters. No wonder the Mizos did not show any enthusiasm to the proposal of Phizo asking them to join hands with the Nagas to fight against India for independence and to form a combined independent state of Naga and Mizo Hills with the Mizo language as the *lingua franca*. The Mizos were, *ad interim*, content with the Autonomous District Council for Mizo Hills and representation by three members in the Assam Legislative Assembly.

The turning-point came in 1959 when the Mizo Hills were hit by a most severe famine. It is commonly believed that the Government of Assam was neither able to assess the seriousness of the impending famine nor could it rise to the occasion in dealing with it. As a result the relief measures were deplorably inadequate, or at least they were perceived to be so by the sufferers. In such matters perception is far more important than reality *per se*. This sowed the seeds of resentment which eventually came to be directed against the Government of India. First the Mizo National Famine Front (MNFF) was formed. By the time the famine was over, it was overwhelmed by political considerations and converted itself into the Mizo National Front (MNF). This also marked the emergence of Lal Denga on the political horizon. He thoroughly exploited the susceptibility and fresh indignation of the famine sufferers, unemployed youth and ex-armymen *et al.*

From December 12, 1962 Lal Denga embarked upon the path of armed struggle for the 'sovereign independence of Greater Mizoram.' The armed wing of the MNF was called Mizo National Volunlteers (MNV). Five years later this was to be rechristened as the Mizo National Amly (MNA). The MNV went about collecting 'taxes' and establishing hide outs. They also established contacts with the Pakistani authorities in East Pakistan. Lal Denga was arrested in December 1963 when he was trying to cross over to East Pakistan. But unfortunately our politicians have shown a very peculiar propensity for repeating their follies. The sordid drama witnessed in the cases of Sheikh Abdullah and Phizo was enacted once again in the case of Lal Denga. He was released in early 1964 itself. The MNF continued to consolidate itself–weapons were procured from East Pakistan and its cadres were trained there. And then he struck!

It was March 1, 1966. The Government was in for the most unkind surprise to find the MNV insurgents launching raids on almost all the security posts simultaneously all over the Mizo Hills. That was Operation Jericho in action. Readers may themselves judge the efficiency of the Indian intelligence machinery. Such a huge operation involving thousands of. insurgents had to be planned for quite some time and the logistics arrangements too must have taken a considerable amount of time, money and the collective effort of so many people. Any intelligence network worth its name should have been able to get a whiff of that. But our intelligence system which specialises only in churning out merely regurgitated garbage produced by the incompetent for the consumption of the insouciant after ingesting untold amount of the alleged secret service fund was gloriously, blissfully unaware of even the minutest part of the tail of all those momentous preparations! In any case retaliatory action was taken and the insurgents fell back on hit and run tactic after hiding in the dense forests.

Mizoram was granted Union Territory status on January 21, 1972 and subsequently the State Assembly election was also held. It is believed that Lal Denga did not cut off his secret communication channels with the Government and maintained his devious links through covert means. It is difficult to make an educated guess about the tangible results of this cloak and-dagger game as it falls into the realm of state secrets and intelligence operations. *Prima facie,* however, it emerges as yet another case of failure as in gradually the insurgency came to stabilise itself. Attacks on security forces, prominent persons and surrendered insurgents continued besides the robberies and the extortions. While the popular support dwindled, the movement succeeded in keeping itself alive by sheer terrorism. In fact the Mizo insurgents are credited with some of the most sensational strikes in the history of insurgent movements in India, one particularly notorious incident among them being the killing of one IGP, one DIG and one SP together right inside the office of the IGP.

Meanwhile things continued to take place in their due course and time. The insurgency, albeit on a lower key, refused to get wiped off. Brig. Sailo (retired) formed a political party called People's Conference and went on to become the Chief Minister. Readers should find it interesting to learn that the son of Brig. Sailo had joined the MNA as a self-styled lieutenant even while Brig. Sailo was in service in the Indian army. Lal Denga, on the other hand, was unrelenting in his secret parleys. Finally, the Government of India relented and made the overture of inviting him to Delhi in January 1976 for open negotiations.

Thus began the series of one of the longest negotiations in the history of the country. They dragged on for more than ten years and witnessed a number of failures in between. The problem lay basically in the desire of Lal Denga to be able to control both the underground as well as the overground elements. The fact was that his influence over the underground leaders in the Arakan Hills who had, *sans* Lal Denga, sustained the insurgency for so long, was waning. More or less the same held true in respect of the overground leaders also. Thus Lal Denga was obliged to shift his position repeatedly in order to placate both the groups and, at the same time, ensure the maximum benefit for himself in the negotiations. The arduous negotiations came to an end in July 1986 when Lal Denga finally signed the Accord with the Government.

Mizo-Chakma Ethnic Conflict

As stated earlier, the Accord has not been violated so far. Socio-political tensions are occasionally generated in the state when the demand for autonomy by tribes like the Hmras, Paithers, Reangs and Chakmas does flare up. That also accounts for the intermittent anti-foreigner agitations by the Mizos. Though the Hmras were placated to some extent in August 1997 by the formation of the Singlung Hill Development Council, some of the disgruntled elements are keeping in touch with the NSCN (I/M).

Then there is the problem of the Mizo-Chakma ethnic conflict The Mizo chauvinists are not pleased with the creation of the Chakma Autonomous District Council (CADC) in 1972. These elements and the members of a student organisation called Mizo Zirlai Pawl (MZP) have also been expressing resentment over the problem of the Chakma refugees from Bangladesh. The matter came to a head with the revision of the electoral rolls in 1994. The Rajya Sabha Committee on Petitions (RSPC) recommended, *inter alia,* granting of Indian citizenship to those Chakmas who had come before March 1971 and also to those who were born in India, while according them the status of Scheduled Tribes. It also recommended an enlargement of the area of the CADC besides placing it under a suitable central agency with proportionate developmental funds at its disposal. In spite of the fact that these recommendations were not implemented, the Mizos got quite incensed. Some of them have gone to the extent of demanding abrogation of the Autonomous District Council (ADC).

The Mizos are having some problems with the Reangs too. The Reangs are demanding an ADC, which the Mizos do not approve of. In October 1997 a Mizo was murdered in a Reang-dominated area. In retaliation the Mizos resorted to large scale arson and did it with such brutal efficiency that about 41,000 Reangs were forced to flee to Tripura and Assam. Now the Mizos are manipulating to ensure that they are not able to return to Mizoram. Against this backdrop it is not surprising that the Reangs too have formed a terrorist outfit called Bru National Liberation Front (BNLF). Ultimately all such outfits come to vent their ire on the Government and the security forces. Recently the BNLF has been suspected of some daring ambushes on security forces inflicting sizeable casualties. It is also suspected that the BNLF has developed links with the National Liberation Front of Tripura. This is a disturbing development.

Although peace has returned to Mizoram, we simply cannot afford, any complacency. There is still a continuous traffic of Myanmar insurgents and non-insurgents along the Indo-Myanmar border. The active groups include the Chin National Front (CNF), the Arakan Liberation Party (ALP) and the National Unity Party of Arakan (NUPA). This traffic is intimately linked with our strategic interests in the area. Further, because of the proximity of Mizoram to Nagaland, Tripura, Assam and Manipur, even Indian insurgents of various groups use the international border along Mizoram for ingress into and egress out of Myanmar.

9

Terrorism in Punjab and Bihar

Sikh Terrorism

Among all the episodes of terrorism that have plagued this country till date, Sikh terrorism was perhaps the most rabidly savage. There was no act of terrorism one could think of that was not perpetrated by the Sikh terrorists with the utmost vehemence. From selective killings to mass killings; from assassinations of prominent persons to subversion of the pseudo-intellectuals; from kidnappings to extortions; from abuse of places of worship to rape committed on the women of those who gave them shelter; from arsons to blowing up of railway tracks; from lootings of banks to obtaining support from the ISI; from transistor bomb explosions to remote-controlled devices; from subversion of petty officials to that of high-ranking officers of the police and the military; from hijacking of aircraft to the destruction of an Air India Jumbo jet; and from ambushes on police patrols to fighting pitched battles with the army, there was perhaps no trick in the arsenal of a terrorist that was not tried by them. Still the movement could never go beyond the stage of pure terrorism. The cry for Khalistan could never enthuse the Sikh masses at large. Besides the religious fanatics and political opportunists, it found its supporters in India only among some pseudo-intellectuals and the *nouveau riche.* The real inspiration for the demand came from the drawing rooms of the wealthy Sikhs who were ensconced in the USA, UK, Canada and Germany. The entire episode of Sikh terrorism is also illustrative of the fact that unless the terrorists are professionals *pur sang,* even terrorism cannot be sustained for long, the financial support of the chauvinist friends abroad and the material support of foreign intelligence agencies like the ISI notwithstanding–some sort of popular support for the cause is necessarily required if a movement is to survive for long. In the case of Sikh terrorism, the Sikh masses could never deny the fact that given their dispersal all over the country, their interests, economic or otherwise, were inextricably linked with the rest of the country. In spite of the shocking experience of the November 1984 riots, there was no sensible Sikh who could confute this cruel logic. The Sikh community did not possess the essential advantage of geographical isolation like the Kashmiris, the Nagas or the Manipuris. Hence an insurgency had to be ruled out from the very beginning as a *non sequitur.* A very determined band of fanatics could, at best, hope for a stretched phase of terrorism. However, in the absence of popular support, this was bound to get reduced to a purely law and order problem which could not withstand the onslaught of a resolute police action. All it needed was the resolve to uproot it. Once the resolve was mustered, the terrorists had no *locus standi* to exploit the use of certain means by the police which were not very honourable, because by that time they had perpetrated enough mayhem to make them lose even a modicum of sympathy from the people. Admittedly, the offensive of the police and the security forces came rather late, but the advantage was that the terrorists could not blunt it by screaming of human rights violations.

Growth of Terrorism in Punjab

Punjab was not one of the backwaters of the country, having any trouble in communications or transport. Thus whatever happened in Punjab was within the full and immediate knowledge of the Government. Yet the total impunity with which the terrorists were able to operate for so long, is a singularly depressing commentary on the political will of the then leadership to combat terrorism. Once again the soft state was found to indulge in the wishful thinking that the problem would somehow go away by itself. Once again it failed miserably in analysing the problem in a correct perspective. Once again it failed to assess the way things were likely to develop. There was devilry in the wind; the atmosphere was charged with seditious talks made all the more fiery by the traditional machismo of the Jat Sikhs–the intelligence machinery could, however, furnish no illuminating analyses of the dominating trends.

The people who were hatching conspiracies; the people who had long been under the influence of seditious leaders like Giani Bakshish Singh of Birmingham, needed only a pretext to unleash a reign of terror. The opportunity presented itself on April 13, 1978. The orthodox Sikhs had a theological difference of opinion with another sect of the Sikhs called the Nirankaris. The Sikh high priests had issued a 'hukamnama' or religious edict, denouncing the Nirankaris as heretics. On that fateful day the Nirankaris were allowed to hold a convention in Amritsar. The fundamentalists objected to that and marched out in a procession shouting slogans against the Nirankaris. The procession was led by Jarnail Singh Bhindranwale and one agriculture inspector Fauja Singh. Thus the incident was also to mark one of the first important acts of terrorism by Bhindranwale. When the procession reached the convention site, Fauja Singh drew his sword and charged at the Nirankari guru, Baba Gurcharan Singh. Fauja Singh was promptly shot dead by one of the bodyguards of Baba Gurcharan. Singh. In the melee and the police firing that ensued 12 Sikhs and three Nirankans were killed.

It can be easily discerned that the whole affair was planned. Fauja Singh was not overcome by some frenzy at the very last moment to make him draw his sword and charge at the Baba. Bhindranwale and his men knew it well that the Baba was protected. They also knew that there was sufficient police deployment at the convention site. Yet they indulged in what they did simply because they wanted a precipitous course of events to take place. As the leftist terrorists had exploited the police firings at Prasadjote (Naxalban) and Indravalli (Andhra Pradesh), so did the Akalis, who accused the Government for having failed to protect the Sikh faith. Thereafter, the acrimony went on building up, along with the lawlessness committed by the fundamentalists.

Baba Gurcharan Singh was finally murdered on April 24, 1980. The bright day was done and Punjab was in for the dark. The response of the administration was absolutely irresolute. An armed desperado belonging to the group of Bhindranwale and the Akhand Kirtani Jatha of Bibi Amarjit Kaur went on a spree of hunting the Nirankaris and all those who dared to criticise them. Meanwhile, the Akalis organised a World Sikh Convention at Amritsar on July 26, 1981 under the presidentship of Sant Harchand Singh Longowal. The convention warned the Government to stop the maltreatment of the Sikhs and threatened a 'Dharma Yuddh' (crusade) in consequence.

Five days later a huge procession was taken out in Amritsar in which, *inter alia*, the status of Holy City was demanded for Amritsar. The situation reached a turning-point when the goons of Bhindranwale murdered Lala Jagat Narain on September 9,1981. Lalaji was a highly respected figure. His paper, the 'Punjab Kesari' had been very bold in criticising the fundamentalists. The Government was obliged to arrest Bhindranwale on September 20, 1981. The terrorists retaliated by several strikes. Rallies were held and processions were taken out in which pro-Khalistani slogans were openly shouted. Once again petty political interests took precedence over national interest. Once again, the lack of foresight was glaringly evident. It seems that there was nobody in the leadership capable of taking a comprehensive view of the problem and react rationally. The administration, in this period, did not come down heavily on the terrorists. The nation seemed to have been paralysed. When it comes to an unfortunate course of events, history has a compulsive way of repeating itself. The Indian State which had blundered in Kashmir, Nagaland and Mizoram was irresistibly drawn into the most ignominious act of unconditionally releasing Bhindranwala in less than a month's time on October 18, 1981. Whatever might have been the motives behind it; whatever might have been the third-rate intelligence input behind it, the fact remains that it turned out to be one of the most catastrophic blunders in the history of terrorism in India. Bhindranwale was, almost overnight, catapulted to the status of a great leader, far more than what he really was. He never looked back after that. Thenceforth, his speeches were to attract large crowds at the Chowk Mehta gurudwara where he spewed venom against the Government, the Nirankaris and the Hindus. The All India Sikh Students Federation (AISSF) under the leadership of Amrik Singh metamorphosed itself into the strong arm of Bhindranwale. Machismo of the most absurd kind had always been the way of life for many Sikh youth-under the influence of Bhindranwale it became a matter of creed. Carrying an AK rifle became the ultimate prestige symbol.

Bhindranwale was shrewd enough to systematically exploit the weaknesses of the system was feeble enough to permit him to do so. As terrorist activities spread their tentacles, Bhindranwale shifted his headquarters from Gurudwara Chowk Mehta to Nanak Niwas in the Golden Temple complex on July 19, 1982.

Bhindranwale sought to counter the move of the Government by moving into the Akal Takht from the Nanak Niwas on December 15, 1983. This should make an interesting study for the scholars of insurgency and counterinsurgency operations. This shows that after all Bhindranwale was no good in the professional business or terrorism. As could well be expected from his background and intellectual capability, he was a classic case of a perfectly medieval mindset. That the AKs had replaced the swords really made no difference as far as the approach to battle was concerned. Bhindranwale committed two strategic mistakes in deciding to continue operating from the Akal Takht. Firstly, he failed to assess how far he could go too far–perhaps he thought that a paralysed system would remain paralysed forever. Secondly, his medieval mindset assured him that he could fight from a 'fort.' That, in essence was his undoing. In fact that violated the very basic principles of terrorism. A terrorist must never fight from a 'fort.' Even in the medieval age, there was usually a limit up to which a fort could be defended. For a terrorist or a guerrilla with limited resources, contesting a ground must be the ultimate taboo. He is not supposed to engage superior forces. Had Bhindranwale been an intelligent terrorist he should have thought of finding some way to escape to Pakistan and direct the operations from there. But that was not expected of him and his advisers, even if they had been modern day senior army officers. Like every thing else in the modern world, if one has to be a terrorist, he must be a good professional terrorist. One can whip up a frenzy en religious fanaticism exploiting the innate susceptibilities of some people–however, one cannot make good professionals out of them. On an intellectual plane, Bhindranwale and his supporters were still in the 17th century.

Operation Blue Star

There was a colossal failure of military intelligence in assessing the ramifications of Operation Blue Star and its repercussions among the Sikh armymen. Not only that military intelligence failed, even the middle level army officers in direct and daily contact with the soldiery displayed such an utter lack of rapport with their men which was acutely redolent of the attitude of the British officers just before the Sepoy Mutiny of 1857. Throughout this work we have tried to emphasise that both at operational and policy making level this nation suffers from a serious crisis of knowledge. So poor was the knowledge of the entire government machinery about the whole phenomenon of insurgency that they completely failed in assessing the impact of Operation Blue Star. Had they possessed an intimate knowledge of the basic driving forces of a seditious movement had they possessed a keen perception of history; and had they possessed a knowledge of the human factors of insurgency, it should have been possible for any sincere intelligence officer to predict that an operation on the Golden Temple would incite religious susceptibilities among the soldiery. Unfortunately we never had such officers. Even now we have only such intelligence officers for whom the job of intelligence ends with making notes befitting junior clerks and statistical statements. There is not a single man with perception at any level.

Readers should be able to recall that nearly 4,000 Sikh soldiers at eight different places had risen in revolt. They assaulted and even killed their officers, looted their armouries, commandeered army vehicles and drove in a mad race to Amritsar. It was a commendable task on the part of the police and the army to intercept them, engage them when necessary and ultimately arrest them. The eight places were thousands of miles apart, ranging from Agartala to Pune, and Ramgarh (Bihar) to Ganganagar (Rajasthan) and Jammu. Yet the pattern of behaviour was almost the same at all the places. If one suggests that it was the outcome of a deep-rooted conspiracy with some foreign hand behind it, military intelligence is to be squarely blamed for the fiasco. If such an extensive conspiracy could be hatched and executed with such perfection, it could only mean that military intelligence was incompetent beyond imagination. If it was a spontaneous reaction then the blame goes squarely on all those junior, middle and senior level officers who while away their time in the cantonments obsequiously pursuing their superiors in the forenoons, playing games in the afternoons and drinking liquor subsidised at the cost of the taxpayers in the evenings. They had maintained no touch with their men, confining themselves to their ivory towers in exactly the same fashion in which the racially arrogant British officers once used to confine themselves. If they do interact with their men at all, it is largely farcical–the interaction being of the most superficial variety, or at best being so condescendingly ceremonious as to render it of no use at all–the archaic tradition of the so-called 'Bara Khana' being a prime example.

This mutiny once again underscores the extreme necessity of maintaining a constant vigil on the religious sensitivities, idiosyncrasies, personal weaknesses, political preferences and the ambitions of all the security forces personnel in general and the army/police officers in particular. If this sounds like turning ours into some sort of police state, so be it. The nation cannot afford the cost of traitorous elements in the army and the police. As long as the Soviet Union had existed, the KGB had done a very thorough job in this direction. There ought to be no shame in learning from their methods and experiences. Furthermore, it goes without saying that such a vigil ought to be continued even after the retirement of the persons concerned.

Decline of Terrorism in Punjab

By 1988 the terrorists again infiltrated the Golden Temple complex. Once again an operation to clear the complex became necessary. This operation, codenamed Black Thunder-II, was undertaken by the National Security Guards (NSG) troops. It differed materially from Operation Blue Star. In the first place the number of terrorists inside was far less, and there were no significant fortifications either. Secondly, they lacked the fatalistic resolve of Bhindranwale and his men. Thirdly, the egregious example of Operation Blue Star was in front of them. Against this backdrop, the terrorists showed no inclination to fight till the last and surrendered. We maintain that the second infiltration of the Golden Temple complex ought to be treated as an aberration; the degree of threat posed this time was far less severe.

Throughout this work we have strongly propounded the theory that the impact of terrorism/insurgency or the anti-terrorist/anti-insurgency drives ought not to be examined in terms of statistical figures alone. Both of them have an important psychological or human component which is not explained by mere figures. Once the nation displayed the resolve to combat terrorism at any cost, terrorist strikes, however sensational, ceased to exercise any effect on the overall tempo. Thus the assassinations of Mrs. Gandhi (October 31, 1984) and Harchand Singh Longowal (August 20, 1985) could not decelerate the process of combating terrorism. Even at the operational level of the police and the para-military forces, a higher number of terrorist strikes did not translate into a corresponding demoralisation in the ranks. Thus it did not matter much that in 1989 there were 1,827 incidents involving a loss of 1,396 lives. It did not matter much that in 1990 terrorists were able to kill 1,970 civilians and 505 personnel of the security forces. What mattered was the fact that the police were no longer demoralised, and that they had gone on the offensive. The fight was taken to the terrorists. They lost 505 men but, at the same time, they were able to kill 1,309 terrorists in return. Night patrolling was done earlier also. However, when Operation Night Dominance was launched, it was a loud pronouncement to the terrorists that the police was no longer apprehensive of the night ambushes; that the police was keen to assert itself; and that the police was out there to hunt the terrorists. Once the security forces got into the right frame of mind and approach, the ultimate demise of terrorism was a foregone conclusion. We have already discussed the intrinsic weaknesses of terrorism in Punjab.

At first, they were able to ride the wave of religious frenzy; then they were fuelled by foreign support, but their base always remained hollow. They were able to thrive for some time because the opposition offered was characterised by vacillation and prostration at the policy making as well as at the operational level. Once that deficiency was made up, terrorism as a serious systemic threat to the body politic of India disappeared fast into the pages of history. The Punjab experience provides valuable lessons to the scholars of Insurgency and Counterinsurgency Operations. Above all, it demonstrates the tragic consequences of the lack of political sagacity. Can the nation forget the way in which Bhindranwale was allowed to attain those monstrous heights? Eventually there was nothing so very novel or great about the Rajiv-Longowal Accord. Most of the provisions in the agreement were informally agreed to several times by the government, but were never executed on one pretext or the others. It needed only some political will to give them a formal shape.

Systemic diseases require systemic treatments. Terrorism in Punjab was not a systemic problem. The eruptions were essentially superficial in character–a topical application of the medication to take care of the invading organisms, followed by some emollient was enough to bring them under control.

Terrorism in Bihar

Since long the socio-economic milleu in Bihar, in terms of caste divide, social exploitation, economic disparity among various social groups, a history of caste conflicts, improper implementation of land reforms, corruption in developmental activities, and above all, an insouciant police response of an *ad hoc* nature, has provided a ground conducive for the nurturance of anti-establishment rebellious thoughts. Leftist terrorists have taken full advantage of it. Readers must realise that when we speak of poverty, it is not merely a hollow word that echoes frequently during seminars of the pseudos or the bureaucrats and that end with sumptuous lunches. A complete description of the state of poverty (euphemistically called economic backwardness in bureaucratic and political circles) and economic disparity in Bihar is beyond the scope of this book. Nevertheless, we should cite a small but very typical example to illustrate the point. A labourer, bonded or unbonded, should normally be obliged to work at the farm of some landlord, or tend to his cattle. It need not be explained that either he has no land of his own or that his small land holding is economically not a viable proposition. For working as a farm labourer he is not likely to receive any wages in cash. Readers should be enlightened to note that there are several laws in the country which are meant essentially to adorn the statute books. Zamindari was abolished a long time back; still some people have managed to manipulate the laws in such a way that landlords still exist all over the country. Similarly, though bonded labour was also declared illegal quite some time back; it still exists very much not only in Bihar but elsewhere too. Those who do not know these stark realities are ignorant; those who refuse to accept the realities are insolent too. There is no dearth of people who were forced to take a loan of just a couple of thousands of rupees for a marriage or some serious sickness. Now since their earnings do not come in cash, they would never be in a position to repay even a fraction of the loan. Thus a vicious circle is established. They have to become bonded labourers because they have to repay the loan. However, despite being bonded labourers, the time would never come when they would be able to repay the loan simply because they are not paid their wages in cash and the wages in kind are so limited that they are barely enough for survival. A typical farm labourer in such areas gets about 17 quintals of paddy and 1.5 quintals of wheat for working round the year. Readers must note the emphasis on the use of words 'in such areas.' We are very much aware of the difference in wages in different areas. However, the figures quoted pertain to the average rate found in the areas affected by leftist terrorism.

The position of the unbounded labourers does not differ markedly for the simple reason that their own land holdings are not economically viable–the cost of irrigation and fertilisers, etc. effectively neutralises the value of the limited produce. The only difference in their case is that they are free to go to Calcutta to pull rickshaws, resulting in a dislocated life which is nearly as bad. Now for the 17 quintals of paddy, it must be kept in mind that one quintal of paddy, when properly dried, gets reduced to about 80 kg. When this is husked, it yields about 60 kg of rice. Thus one labourer gets actually about 1,020 kg of rice and 150 kg of wheat in one year. This comes to 97.5 kg of foodgrains per month. Now for a family of nine members (two adults and seven children–that is the average size of a family in those parts; so much for the family planning programmes) the average consumption of foodgrains comes to 190 kg per month. Readers should not be surprised at that. These people survive on rice and rice alone; the staple diet being rice and salt. Pulses and vegetables cannot even be dreamt of. Thus it should require two full-time workers to earn the grains for the food for survival. Since the woman cannot afford to be a full-time worker, this means that several children are to be pooled in just to earn the necessary food on which they have to survive. Any other necessity of life, even if it is something important as medical treatment at the hands of some quack, demands that it should be met from yet another loan. Not only that, we have found that some landlords are bringing (or threatening to bring) labourers from some other parts of the district or neighbouring districts so as to keep the local labourers off work and ultimately force them to accept work for even lesser wages. Landlords are not the only exploiters. Another important category is forest officials. In the tribal belts where even farm labour is not easily available, the tribals survive basically on jungle produce. There they are at the mercy of the forest officials. For making 100 packets of tendu leaves, they pay only about Rs. 24 or so per day. When it comes to social forestry plantation work, the workers are given so unrealistic targets that against a theoretically attainable wage of Rs. 47 per day, they never get more than Rs. 30. A similar exploitation is resorted to by the contractors also. Add, occasional sexual exploitation by the goons of these people and you get a picture which is not very different from the one painted in the pamphlets of the terrorists.

These exploited people form the ground which provides sympathy and shelter to the terrorists, even if they do not have any organisational structure in the area. It becomes only a matter of time before they strike root. Terrorists are always on lookout for those people who are thoroughly fed up with the existing state of exploitation and their abject poverty. Those of them who have some amount of courage and self-respect, cross the Rubicon and take up arms. Usually it requires only some particularly appalling incident of violence or sexual exploitation to trigger a wave of sympathy for the terrorists. This wave is so forceful that those who were so far providing only shelter to the terrorists, and sometimes that too under some coercion, decide to join their ranks. One requires only that last effort to free himself from the traditional bonds of the family. He knows that life with the terrorists would indeed be tough, but life in the village is not much better either.

Leftist terrorism in Bihar was continued by the Maoist Communist Centre (MCC), the Central Organising Committee-CPML-Party Unity (PU) and the CPML-Anti-Lin Biao faction of Vinod Mishra.

After the death of Kanai Chatterjee in 1982, the MCC found two dynamic leaders in the form of Pramod Mishra and Sanjay Dusadh. Under them, the influence of the MCC increased considerably through front organisations like Krantikari Kisan Committee, Jan Suraksha Sangharsh, Manch, Krantikari Buddhijeevi Sangh and Krantikari Chhatra League. It should, however, not be forgotten that much of the ground sympathetic to the leftists was created by the general poverty, tardy implementation of land reforms and the unsympathetic or callous attitude of the administration towards the misery of the lower classes in Bihar.

The violence perpetrated by these groups needs no elaboration. Anybody who reads newspapers or watches T.V. must be sick of them. The violence is still characterised by a high degree of brutality in the sense of mass killings, dismemberment, and not sparing of the women or children.

Defending Our Society

Concern to protect and defend the basic opennes of our society has led to restrictions on the gathering of intelligence, particularly about Americans, and to intense pressures for the disclosure of government documents. Past abuses of power may have generated these pressures, but the results have not always contributed to a sound counter-terrorist programme. As long as the terrorist threat remains low in the United States, these restrictions will be appropriate. But were there to be a major upsurge in terrorist violence, we could not expect to have substantial amounts of information about its perpetrators. The opening of government files under Freedom of Information procedures also has had the unexpected consequence of restricting the flow of information between governments. Our closest friends have begun to lose confidence in our ability to protect their secrets. We must be concerned not to overreact to hypothetical dangers. We always must be concerned to protect our basic civil rights. But we also must be sure that we have not excessively diminished our capacity to deal with the real threat which terrorism represents.

As we look to the future, we must anticipate ever more complex and demanding situations against which our policy will be judged. Iran is a case in point. Terrorists may choose new weapons, such as surface-to-air missiles, rockets, chemical, biological or even nuclear agents. They may choose new targets focusing on the many vulnerabilities of modern industrial civilization: power generation and transmission facilities, tankers, pipelines, computers. If they do, we must be prepared.

In such situations we need to strike a careful balance among our various interests. We will need to use all our resources imaginatively. Because terrorism always raises complex political and moral issues, the agenda for future action will be long. Prevention, deterrence, reaction, and prediction should be the hallmarks of our policy. In each area, we will need to have a clear understanding of the terrorist and his motives. It is here that the contribution of the psychiatrist and the psychologist is most relevant. The more we understand about the psychopathology of terrorism and assassination, the more effective we will be in predicting its occurrence, in deterring its perpetrators, in devising appropriate tactics, and in focusing our reaction against it. This is a task on which we are all embarked and where the world of academia and government meet on common ground.

10

Technology Used in Terrorism

Modern Terrorism

Modern terrorism, with sophisticated technological means at its disposal and the future possibility of access to biological and nuclear weapons, presents a clear and present danger to the very existence of civilization itself. Such as awesome eventuality forces us to think about the 'unthinkable' with grave concern. The purpose of this chapter is to examine these novel aspects of contemporary ideological and political violence and to focus on the potential threat of nuclear terrorism.

Pragmatic and symbolic terrorist acts–arson, bombing, hostage taking, kidnapping, and murder–undertaken by extremist groups for the purpose of pressuring governments and peoples to concede to the demands of the perpetrators already have victimized, killed, and maimed thousands of innocent civilians. These casualties include government officials, politicians, judges, diplomats, military personnel, police officers, business executive, labour leaders, university professors, college students, school children, travellers, pilgrims, and Olympic athletes. Considerable damage has been inflicted as well on nonhuman targets. Terrorists have attacked government offices and police stations; pubs, restaurants, and hotels; banks, supermarkets, and department stores; oil pipelines, storage tanks, and refineries; railroad stations, air terminals, and jetliners; broadcasting stations, computer and data centres, and electrical power facilities.

No mass casualties and widespread disruptions to vital systems of industrialized nations have yet resulted from a single terrorist attack. Terrorist groups usually have used guns and bombs and, only rarely, more sophisticated weapons such as man-portable antitank rockets and ground-to-air missiles when they became available. Having achieved considerable tactical success, terrorists have found it politically and morally expedient to restrain the level of violence. Had it been otherwise, they could have used conventional weapons to cause major disasters in our extremely vulnerable society by attacking, for example, hazardous-chemical plants.

There are, however, no guarantees that the self-imposed constraints of terrorist groups will persist indefinitely and that future incidents will not be much more costly in terms of human lives and property. Three considerations suggest such a probable draconian development. First, assuming that conventional terrorism would be brought under substantial control in the foreseeable future through national and international legislation, as we as through increased security and enforcement measures, this, in fact, may hasten the advent of mass destruction terrorism. After all, terrorist groups tend, whenever possible, to attack 'soft' targets, those without security or any appearance thereof. This worldwide trend has been noted clearly over the 1970–78 time span and accounts for an evolution in terrorist targeting from the primacy accorded attacks on police and military facilities (1970–72), to a shift toward assaulting diplomatic and related personnel (1973–75), to an emphasis on business targets (1976–78).

Today, however, many business firms are following the lead of police and diplomatic establishments by upgrading their security. As a result, other vulnerable targets created by technological advances of contemporary society are likely to become more attractive to terrorists.

It is clear that the prospects of success for such a group would be enhanced if it had previously demonstrated high technological capabilities and a strong willingness to incur high risk involved in similar ventures. Even if there were some skepticism about the credibility of the threat, no rational government would lightly risk a non-conventional incident. The danger here is that if one subnational body succeeds in achieving its goals, then the temptation for other terrorist groups to us, or threaten to use, similar weapons may become irresistible.

Weapons of High Technology

There are inherent differences, to be sure, among weapons of high technology with regard to their characteristics and modes of action. The resort to chemical and biological weapons is more achievable than the use of nuclear explosives; more specifically, no insurmountable technological impediments arise in the utilization of chemical agents (*e.g.*, fluoroacetates, organophosphorous compounds, and botulinum toxin). They are relatively easy to obtain, their delivery systems are manageable, and their dispersal techniques are efficient. For example, it has recently been reported that 'terrorist wanting to make deadly nerve gases can still find the formulas at the British Library despite attempts by the government to remove them from public access.'

Once in possession of such information, a terrorist with some technical know-how could synthesize toxic chemical agents from raw materials or intermediates. In fact, many chemical toxins (*e.g.*, cobalt 60 and TEPP insecticides) are commercially available; they could be either bought or stolen. Also, covert and overt options for dispersing chemical agents are virtually limitless: the poisoning of water systems, contamination of food supplies, generation of gases in enclosed spaces with volatile agents, generation of aerosols in enclosed spaces with nonvolatile agents, and dispersal with explosives.

A number of chemical terrorism incidents already have occurred. In 1975, German authorities received the threat that mustard gas, stolen from an ammunition bunker in the country would be used against the population of Stuttgart unless all political prisoners were granted immunity. Only some of the stolen canisters were later found. In the following years, US postal authorities intercepted a package, presumably mailed by an Arab terrorist group, containing a small charge designed to explode a vial of nerve gas when the package was opened. And more recently, Israeli citrus fruit was contaminated with liquid mercury.

As in the case of chemical violence, biological terrorism–the use of living organisms to cause disease or death in man, animals, or plants–is technologically possible. Warfare agents such as brucellosis (undulant fever), coccidioidomycosis (San Joaquin Valley or desert fever), and psittacosis (parrot fever) are easy to acquire, cultivate, and disseminate. The poison ricin, for example, is developed from castor beans; only about half a milligram is fatal.

Evidence indicates that terrorists seriously have considered resorting to biological terrorism. In 1970, members of the Weather Underground were planning to steal germs from the Bacteriological Warfare Centre at Fort Detrick, Maryland, for the purpose of contaminating a city water supply; organizers of Rise, a group of young people dedicated to creating a new master race, were arrested in 1972 in an abortive plot to poison Chicago's water system with typhoid bacteria; and in 1975 technical military manuals on germ warfare were found in a San Francisco hideout of the Symbionese Liberation Army.

Notwithstanding the assumption that in the short-term future chemical and biological terrorism is more feasible technologically, nuclear terrorism–the explosion of a nuclear bomb, the use of fissionable material as a radioactive poison, and the seizure and sabotage of nuclear facilities–has received far greater public attention. As one observer remarked, 'It cannot be assumed that these possibilities have been ignored by existing or potential terrorists or that they will not be considered the future.'

Awareness of this danger is growing. Warnings were issued in the United States and abroad that thefts from nuclear plants might provide terrorist with material to make a crude bomb. Concern also was expressed that the attacks on nuclear power plants discussed in European underground publications may encourage domestic groups to escalate their violence. And more recently, Joseph M.

Hendrie, Chairman of the Nuclear Regulatory Commission, reported that his 'agency has concluded (that) he possibility of terrorist interest in nuclear capability cannot be discounted.'

Scholars have provided numerous scenarios of nuclear terrorism over the years. Examples of some of the more obvious possibilities that are technically feasible and politically plausible include the threat or use of a nuclear option by: a group of psychopaths and socio paths with suicidal tendencies, who use nihilistic violence for its own sake; political of environmental extremists seeking to carry out acts of symbolic violence against nuclear facilities; a revolutionary group acting against its own government or against a foreign country in order to increase pressure on the home government to meet the revolutionaries' demands; a national liberation movement working against the imperalist government in the mother country; or a terrorist group engaged in a proxy war initiated by an outside state or even a nuclear power.

Such developments are indeed serious because they either could result in a broad-scale nuclear war or increase the risk of such a war. This likelihood increases in situations where nuclear terrorism can be used as a form of war by proxy or as a tactical weapon by desperate terrorist groups. It is conceivable, for example, that if Israel were a target of a 'surrogate' nuclear attack by the Palestine Liberation Organization (PLO), the United States and the Soviet Union might reach a point of confrontation that greatly increases the dangers of a nuclear war between them.

A major factor encouraging this frightening reality is the profound negative effects of nuclear proliferation, both vertically and horizontally. At present, tens of thousands of nuclear weapons, including tactical ones, are in military stockpiles. Although the current 'nuclear club' is limited in membership, it is expected that some forty to fifty nations will have access to peaceful nuclear material and technology by the end of the century.

The enormous expansion in the nuclear arsenal is indeed alarming, not only because of the total number of weapons stockpiled but also because most of them will be without the electronic safety locks and coded Permissive Action Links (PALs) protecting weapons of the more advanced nuclear powers. While stealing or seizing a tactical nuclear weapon from a less sophisticated nuclear nation might be more tempting to a terrorist group, an attempt to acquire weapons from the superpowers should not be ruled out. For instance, weaknesses and shortcomings in the security system of some US Armed Forces' storage depots highlight questions of command, inventory control, and communications. Furthermore, the transit of nuclear warheads between missile sites (identifiable storage sites, unsafe transport, etc.) improves the chances for success of a terrorist group. Even if the difficulties of detonation of a stolen bomb prove to be insurmountable, the terrorist group still will be able to use the weapon as a credible threat.

Concern over the risk of theft or seizure of tactical and strategic weapons at home and abroad has been expressed by many observers. One test scenario describes the seizure of a launch control centre at a Minuteman missile site by terrorists, thereby providing them with the capability to launch a nuclear attack. In this particular case, 'there is little reason to have confidence that Minuteman safeguards are inviolable.'

Even if shortcomings in safeguards and physical security measures of the United States and other advanced nuclear countries were corrected, the fact remains that lesser technological states will not always introduce similar improvements, and therefore, they still will be vulnerable to seizure or theft of nuclear weapons. In such circumstances, the security of the more sophisticated nuclear states could well be in jeopardy. Clearly, protection and safety can be improved on all levels, but the risks can only be reduced and not completely eliminated.

As a consequence of the use of the oil embargo and the political unreliability of some oil-producing countries, moreover, industrial nations have been motivated to develop alternative sources of energy. Nuclear power has figured largely in these efforts. Thus, as the world moves deeper into the plutonium economy, the potential dangers of diversion, theft, or seizure of fissionable nuclear material produced by private industry will become greater.

This vulnerability in the United States and elsewhere already has generated various recommendations on international and national levels to improve the physical protection of nuclear material in civilian hands. Cases in point are the reports, suggestions, guidelines, and regulations provided by the International Atomic

Energy Agency (IAEA), the Non-Proliferation Treaty Review Conference, and the US Atomic Energy Commission. Despite these and other efforts, current international safeguards are totally inadequate. Some analysts have concluded that there 'is so systematic exchange among states of technical, administrative, or intelligence information regarding physical protection of nuclear facilities and materials or of information concerning terrorist threat potentials. Similarly, there appears to be no contingency plan for, nor international coordinative mechanism to deal with, a theft of nuclear materials from one state to another.'

This vulnerability is expected to result in the opening up of opportunities for a black market of plutonium, thereby increasing the chances of success in obtaining the needed fissionable material. Only some eleven to twenty pounds of such material are necessary to construct a crude explosive device with a probable yield in the range between several hundreds and several thousands of high explosives. If this device were detonated in a crowded metropolitan area, as many as 10,000 people might be killed directly, while tens of thousands of others might suffer from severe fallout exposure.

With fissionable material available, to be sure, a determined terrorist group wishing to manufacture its own homemade weapon can do so without insurmountable difficulty.

Nuclear Terrorism

If bright undergraduates have the technological know-how to design nuclear bombs, then it is obvious that any proficient terrorist group who can obtain the fissionable material and do what these students have done will have a reasonable chance of building, quite skillfully and safely, a homemade bomb for $ 10,000 to $ 30,000. It is even possible that some of the tens of thousands of scientists, engineers, and other trained personnel in the nuclear field might be motivated by political convictions or economic and personal considerations and therefore participate in a nuclear operation. In addition, experts themselves might be kidnapped and forced to contribute their expertise in exchange for their lives or the lives of their families.

Another aspect of nuclear terrorism is the problem of radiological weapons dispersal. A plausible alternative to the explosion or threat of explosion of a nuclear device is the utilization of plutonium or any other radioactive nuclides for the dispersal of radioactivity in any given area, or for the contamination of natural resources. A dispersal threat would be more credible if only because it requires less material and a lower level of technological expertise. Thus, a determined terrorist group could place only 3½ ounces of plutonium (its toxicity is at least 20,000 times that of cobra venom or potassium cyanide) in a dispersal device such as an aerosol canister. This could be an effective radiological weapon if introduced into the air conditioning system of a large government office building. The result would be devastating. Several thousand people would die over a period of time depending on the level of dosage absorbed. Additionally, significant psychological effects could create immediate panic and spontaneous mass exodus, resulting in intolerable political, economic, and social implications.

Another threat of radioactivity release could occur as a consequence of the sabotage of nuclear power stations. Since an expansion in the number of these stations is expected, the likelihood of such incidents increases. To succeed in such an operation, the terrorists must disable the cooling system to the reactor core of the power station, where radioactive material is contained, thus causing it to melt and release the poisonous substance. Although such a task is more difficult, experts agree that it is not impossible. Once the reactor core melts down, the released material would cause thousands of casualties and serious environmental, contamination with both short-and long-term effects. As one observer of nuclear developments has predicted: 'Because of its toxic and fissile properties, plutonium offers a unique and powerful weapon to those who are sufficiently determined to impose their will. In these circumstances I do not believe it is a question of whether someone will deliberately acquire it for purposes of terrorism and blackmail, but only of when and how often.'

This prediction is not baseless if we examine the historical record. There have already been several hundreds of nuclear-related incidents with serious implications for future trends. Some unclassified examples in the United States, selected at random, include the theft in 1973 of 'extremely harmful' capsules of iodine 131 from a hospital in Arcadia, California; the loss in 1969 of a container of highly enriched uranium hexafluoride (UF–6) which was being shipped from Ohio to Missouri; the 1972 threatened crash of a hijacked airliner into the Oak Ridge National Laboratory in Tennessee; the arson at the Indian Point Unit 2 plant near Buchanan, New York, in 1974; the intrusion attempt in 1977 into the Vermont Yankee Nuclear Power Corp.; the 1976 bomb threat at the B and W naval nuclear fuel facility at Lynchburg, Virginia; and the bomb detonation next to the visitors' centre at the Trojan nuclear power plant in Prescott, Oregon, in 1977. Thus far, thousands of pounds of low-enriched uranium and plutonium have disappeared during the past several years. According to a recent report, more than fifty tons of fissionable material was unaccounted for in some thirty-four facilities operated by the Energy Research and Development Administration.

Since 1970 there have been a dozen terrorist attacks against nuclear facilities. According to available data, these incidents represent 6.8 per cent of the total of 192 terrorist attacks against utilities around the world. For instance, in 1973 members of the Revolutionary Army of the People (Ejircito Revolucionario del Pueblo-ERP) seized the nearly completed Atucha nuclear station in Argentina; the attackers escaped after painting apolitical slogan on the building, stealing weapons, and wounding several guards. In 1975 several bombs exploded at the site of a French nuclear power station under construction in Fessenheim, south of Strasbourg; there was some damage, but no significant delay in the completion of the reactor. The 'Meinhof-Puig Antioch' group claimed credit for this incident. During the same year two explosions caused minor damage to a nuclear power plant in Brittany; a local separatist group has been suspected of this act of sabotage. Other attacks occurred in 1976 when a group known as Commando d'Opposition par Explosifs a I' Auto-destruction de l'Univers (COPEAU)–or Commando of Opposition by Explosives to the Self-Destruction of the Universe-bombed the Paris offices of a manufacturer of nuclear fuel elements and a uranium mine in south western France, causing extensive damage at both locations.

Two incidents are noteworthy. In March 1978, the Basque Separatist Terrorist Organization (ETA) bombed the partially built nuclear plant in Lemoniz, Spain, the second largest in Western Europe; the bombing caused $ 8.1 million in damage to the plant, killed two workers, and injured fourteen. Several months earlier members of the same group had opened fire at the site but were beaten back by police. And in a related nuclear facility issue, the German Revolutionary Cells have claimed responsibility for a May 1978 explosives attack on a private security firm contracting at a nuclear works site at Kalkar, West Germany, and for an incendiary, attack on a vehicle belonging to the police chief who handled violent demonstrations at that location.

Limited as these incidents are, they should not be construed to mean that the world in the years ahead will face only isolated cases of nuclear terrorism. It is likely that changing political, economic, and social patterns in the domestic and international situations over the next few decades might give rise to pressures and tensions that could motivate terrorists to engage in nuclear terrorism.

The intrinsically complicated threats arising from any sort of chemical, biological, and nuclear terrorism may become an ominous future reality. If modern society is to provide a reasonable degree of protection against super-terrorism, developments in this area of public concern must be monitored continuously and patiently by all involved. Emergency preparedness counter-measures necessarily must include contingency planning and sound crisis management policies at various governmental, intergovernmental, and non-governmental levels.

Faced with potential dangers of unconventional terrorism, democratic states must ask themselves what price they are prepared to pay, in terms both of expenditures and of diminution of their citizens' convenience and civil liberties.

11

The Rebellions

Meaning of a Rebellion

One enjoys an analytical advantage in seeking to understand what rebellion means not through explicit normative formulations but through mythologies in which rebellion is represented 'in flesh and blood' (or at least the kind of flesh and blood that mythologies recognize). The advantage is that a mythology, at least a basic mythology of one of the historic civilizations, contains not only a normative principle, but also, and primarily:

1. A model of consciousness for comprehending a particular type of human behaviour.
2. A psychological theory revealing how, and of what materials, a particular cultural tradition constructs psychological theories, and
3. A suggestion of the sociological setting within which either:
   (a) the type of behaviour represented in the myth tends to arise, or
   (b) a particular psychological theory of its genesis and manifestations is generated.

Thus, a mythological representation reveals not only how rebellion was understood in the civilization in which the myth was created and how different understandings of rebellion arise; it also provides one of the general human (that is, inter-civilizational) repertoire in all times and places. It is in this sense that great myths are 'eternally true'–though they are true as *theories* applicable to particular segments of experience, not as overarching *systems* embracing all reality.

Surely what might be called the 'humane attachment–practical assistance mechanism' is a universal possibility, experienced and observed by people in all civilizations. But what is remarkable is that the Greeks–or *some* significant assistance mechanism with what they themselves thought of as precisely, against a concrete inequity in the normative order sanctioned by it. Rebellion is therefore a 'noble crime'; and in the life history of the rebel (or in the historical development of his image) the substantive personal virtue of the individual overcomes the formal criminality of his act.

This is one model for conceptualizing the behaviour of the rebel. The other is the Satanic model. As described in medieval Christian writings Satan rebels out of resentment. The causes of his resentment are variously interpreted by the theologians: he is the first of the angels who thinks he has been replaced in God's affection by a 'younger sibling'–man or Christ; he objects to having been created by someone else and wants to be the sole maker of his own identity. But he rebels not out of sympathy for others, but from resentment of what he perceives as loss or lack of recognition of his own excellence–'pride born of envy' and 'a sense of his own greatness.' And, while he employs wealth and power as a means for attaining control over those he seeks to corrupt, he is wholly unconcerned with meeting the practical (food, warmth or health) needs of anyone.

Indeed, both as the servant of God, in the story of Job, and as the evil one, Satan appears to find the peaceful enjoyment of material comfort intolerable. The simple felicities of ordinary life offend against Satan's single-minded pursuit of absolute 'virtue' or, in his, transformed state, 'anti-virtue.' The final goal of the resentful idealist is to create a total alternative to the divine order, an 'adversary culture' and, within it, to assume God's place. But the results of his activities are wholly destructive. While Prometheus, a materialist-rationalist 'partial rebel' who sought only to provide a useful service, winds up evoking a new conception of justice which even Zeus, in the lost parts of the Aeschylean trilogy, apparently comes to accept-Satan proves unable to create any value and can only mock the old by inverting them. The would be total innovator is enchained to inverse of all of the old.

Satanic behaviour can be conceptualized psychologically as governed by the resentment-destruction mechanism. Surely this mechanism, too, is a universal possibility, experienced and observed by people in all civilizations. But note that in the Judeo-Christian, and particularly the medieval Christian, tradition it is the resentment-destruction mechanism that is finely attached to the theme of rebellion against the legitimately established power holders and the normative order represented by them. Within this tradition, there is no nobility in the crime of rebellion against the existing normative order. Rebellion is itself evil even when its occurrence is 'objectively necessary for the completion of the larger design of God and contributes to the comprehension, by men, of this design. What is 'spontaneous' in Satan is evil even though this spontaneity has been 'provided for' and kept 'under control' by the irreplaceable occupant for the commanding heights of 'power' and 'goodness.'

The connection between rebellion and the resentment–destruction mechanism is much more central to the Christian tradition that the linkage between rebellion and the sympathy–assistance mechanism in the Greek civilization. Prometheus was far less important in Greek mythology than Satan in the medieval Christian. But, centrality aside, the linkage of the cultural theme of rebellion with the psychological mechanism of humane attachment resulting in practical assistance to others is, among the historic civilizations, a distinctively Greek theme. The older Plato would not have appreciated it, but in no other pre-modern civilization has this particular linkage of themes been given a mythological elaboration anywhere approaching that given to it by Aeschylus. And we are concerned not only with what is central to a civilization, but also with what is unique in it.

Moral Thinking about 'Good' and 'Evil'

Within the relatively enduring Indian and Chinese structures of moral thinking, the primary categories to which substance is attributed are not 'good' and 'evil,' and the relationships between the fundamental opposites take the form neither of 'battle' nor of 'dialectical transformation.' In Hinduism, dualistic categories both stand in a relationship of mutual recognition of each other (being in the world and world renunciation) and (as in the purity-pollution distinction) are used to separate hierarchically arranged entities representing phases of an interminably cyclical process. While the categories themselves constitute a permanent structure, the particular contents of Indian categories are comparatively fluid: the ascetic becomes an erotic profligate and bounces back again; an individual moves from being in the world to world renunciation; what is 'polluting' overflows and infects the 'pure' (but never the opposite, thus suggesting the strength of 'pollution' and the weakness of 'purity,' in some contrast to the powerful Chinese belief that good examples normally attract others to emulate them).

In Confucian China, polarities equal in value but unequal in power (as in the Yin-Yang paradigm) cooperate, in a rigorously defined but contextually variable manner, to sustain and develop a harmonious cosmic hierarchy. This is less fluidity of the contents of the categories and more of a 'practical' cooperation between the opposites than in the Indian structure of moral thinking.

In the medieval and early modern European tradition, polar opposites either battle energetically until the final solution the outcome of which is predetermined (the God-Satan model), or are mutually interdependent in a static hierarchical relationship, which it is impermissible to challenge (as in the notion of the 'marriage' of the soul with the body, in which the 'masculine' soul is entitled to the obedience of the 'feminine' body). The result of the concurrent presence of both of these models in the Western tradition is a constant tension between 'herarchy' and 'dualism': hierarchies are always potentially threatened by a dualistic militance subversive of them, as they are not in either India or China.

In contrast to all of these conceptions of the proper relationship between polar opposites, Greek dramatists have conceived of a dialectic in which the opposite evolve, changing their own character and the structure of their setting, in the course of a battle in which the cards are not stacked in advance in favour of one participant, as they are in the God-Satan paradigm. While the image of Prometheus has appealed at various times and in various ways to European traditions of experience, the Promethean dialectic has re-emerged most prominently in the Romantic imagination. But the Romantics had a tendency to collapse Satan and Prometheus into one (or rather to impart the psychological qualities of the former to the imagery of the latter). Marx resonated to this ambience; Stalin remained a medieval Christian dominant with a factory for the transformation of humanity in his hands.

The second approach to explaining the differences between the Greek and the Judeo-Christian models of rebellious behaviour, and between their theories of the origin of such behaviour, can be made on the *social-structural* level. The construction of Satan has started within the general ambience of a militaristic, Persian 'oriental despotism,' where the obligation of everyone, including the highest officials, has been to serve the ruler in the manner of disciplined soldiers, and in which, since the judgement of the supreme power holder could not legitimately be questioned, failure to submit to him had to appear as the upheaval of primeval chaos against the righteousness of civilization. The Persian type of oriental despotism may be contrasted to the bureaucratic empire of historic China, where officials, insofar as they were 'true gentlemen' (chün-tzu), adhered to generalized moral standards of their estate; by which they could define their own dignity and even judge their supreme authority, the emperor–thus retaining a certain margin of dignified moral independence relative to him.

In the Chinese framework, in which supreme worldly power could legitimately be perceived as deficient in knowledge and in virtue, rebellion could not automatically be judged as arising outside of the normative order and as constituting a threat not only to the current political manifestation of that order, but to the principle of order itself.

The most popular image of the rebel in traditional Chinese fiction is that of a trickster–monkey who after having fought successfully against all sorts of heavenly powers and secular sagos, ends up as the defender of a Buddhist pilgrim. Rebelliousness, in this case, appears not as a serious human, angelic or titanic quality, but as a playful expression of primordial nature, capable, in the very course of its rebellion, of rising to the level of moral responsibility. There is a bit of Prometheus in the monkey, but nothing whatsoever of Satan. Actual rebellions tended in China to be rationalized by the theorists as expressions of the loss of 'the mandate of heaven' and legitimated by the rebels themselves, until the nineteenth century, in the imagery of the nature mysticism of popular Taoism and the reassertion of traditional peasant values.

The myth of Prometheus has been put together in a society which cultivated 'individualistic heroism' in social action and in fact provided opportunities for a privileged elite to seek this goal. When Prometheus first appears, in Hesiod, the breaking down of clan controls was taking place in the absence of both a dominant state organization and a rigorously dualistic intellectual culture. In this setting, a mere semi god senses the 'prerogative of the privileged'– the obligation to come to the aid of others in *hiw own* way, without waiting for legitimation by any traditional standard or a newly formulated explicit ideology. A society which permits individualistic practical (not merely symbolic) action for at least some of its members is probably necessary for such trust in one's own private moral sensitivities, not sanctioned by any imaginable agency or tradition external to the individual. In a stable peasant society, or within a bureaucracy such an attitude would not be credible enough to sustain a great myth.

Yet Prometheus is not a feudal lord, or a Hegelian 'honest soul,' acting with the archaic directness of 'honour.' He is a 'subtle-spirit' (Aeschylus), a user of his mind, who has clearly seen oppression and its limits, and it has become his nature to 'think deviously' (Hesiod): it is apparently Prometheus who has invented the deceptive sacrifice to the powerful. But to invent it with full conviction in the propriety of his act, he has not to need it for himself. He is willing to sin, but only for the concrete benefit of others. In the tradition in which he originates, this commitment is associated with supreme intelligence.

Another structural characteristic of the Greek society relevant to the Promethean theme is the presence of a body of intellectuals, principally the dramatic poets, who were deeply concerned with interpreting moral issues, but were not deeply functionaries within, or tightly controlled by, a religious or political organization. In the ancient Near East, where moral poetry was, by and large, in the hands of organized religious bodies, the priesthoods were organized, like the state, along the lines of a militaristic 'oriental despotism.' In the Israelite tradition, where they were not–and where the institution of prophecy permitted 'rebelliousness' against the established social order in the name of a higher obedience, Satan originally did not have the character of a rebel, let alone a nihilistic rebel.

The sense of the virulence of Satan had been taking shape under the Seleucid conquerors of Palestine, when a strong movement toward Hellenization in the Jewish aristocracy, ambitious to increase the scope of its power, began seriously to threaten the cultural identity of the Jewish community.

The analysis of the interpretations of rebellious behaviour underlines the impossibility of understanding the distinctive symbolic designs of particular civilizations *either* without reference to their social structures or as direct reflections of their social structures. Nor, in all likelihood, should differences in symbolic designs be read as registering corresponding differences in visible behaviour, or the absence of a particular symbolic design be interpreted as indicating the absence of the behaviour which other peoples objectify in such designs. What symbolic designs in their totality express exists, outside of them; only in the imagination; and not all the 'raw materials' of experience that exist outside of the active imagination are transmuted into its splendid and horrifying craftsmanship.

Terrorist Outrage

Indeed, each successive terrorist outrage illuminated the government's inability to curb, much less defeat the terrorists. Already sapped by the Second World War, Britain's limited economic resources were further strained by the cost of deploying so large a military force to Palestine to cope with the tide of violence submerging the country. Public opinion in Britain, already ill-dispose to the continued loss of life and expenditure of effort in an unwinnable situation, was further inflamed by incidents such as the King David Hotel bombing and the Irgun's hanging in July 1947 of two sergeants in retaliation for the government's execution of three convicted Irgun terrorists. As the renowned British historian of the Middle East, Elizabeth Monroe, has noted in respect of the hangings: "The British public had taken Palestine in its stride....and had looked upon "disturbances" and "violence" there much as it viewed "the troubles" in Ireland–as an unpleasant experience that was part of the white man's burden." All this changed, however, with the cold-blooded murder of the sergeants. Photographs of the grim death scene-depicting, the two corpses just inches above the ground, the sergeants' hooded faces and bloodied shirts–were emblazoned across the front pages of British newspapers under headlines decrying their execution as an act of 'medieval barbarity.' As inured to the almost daily reports of the death and deprivation suffered by the army in Palestine as the British public was, the brutal execution of the two sergeants made a deep and unalterable impression on the national psyche. "All home comment on that deed," Monroe continued, was "different in tone from that on earlier terrorist acts, many of which caused greater loss of life–for instance, the blowing up of the officers' club or of the King David Hotel." For both the British public and the press, the murders seemed to demonstrate the futility of the situation in Palestine and the pointlessness of remaining there any longer than was absolutely necessary.

The ethno-nationalist insurrections that followed the Second World War had a lasting influence on subsequent terrorist campaigns. Although governments throughout history and all over the world always claim that terrorism is ineffective as and instrument of political change, the examples of Israel, Cyprus and Algeria, and of Begin, Makarios and Ahmed Ben Bella (the FLN's leader, who became Algeria's first President), provide convincing evidence to the contrary. Admittedly, the establishment of these independent countries was both confined to a distinct period of time and the product, in some cases, of powerful forces other than terrorism. At the same time, however, it is indisputable that, at the very least, the tactical 'successes' and political victories won through violence by groups like the Irgun, EOKA and the FLN clearly demonstrated that-notwithstanding the repeated denials of the governments they confronted-terrorism does 'work.' Even if this 'success' did not always manifest itself in terms of the actual acquisition of power in government, the respectability accorded to terrorist organizations hitherto branded as 'criminals' in fora like the United Nations and their success in attracting attention to themselves and their causes, in publicizing grievances that might otherwise have gone overlooked and perhaps even in compelling governments to address issues that, if not for the terrorists' violence, would have largely been ignored, cannot be disregarded.

In sum, the anti-colonial social terrorism campaigns are critical to understanding the evolution and development of modern, contemporary terrorism. They were the first to recognize the publicity value inherent in terrorism and to choreograph their violence for an audience far beyond the immediate geographical loci of their respective struggles. The Irgun directed its message to New York and Washington, DC, as much as to London and Jerusalem. EOKA similarly appealed to opinion in New York and London as well as in Athens and Nicosia. And the FLN was especially concerned with influencing policy not only in Algiers but New York and Paris too. The ability of these groups to mobilize sympathy and support outside the narrow confines of their actual 'theatres of operation' thus taught a powerful lesson to similarly aggrieved peoples elsewhere, who now saw in terrorism an effective means of transforming hitherto local conflicts into international issues. Thus, the foundations were laid for the transformation of terrorism in the late 1960s from a primarily localized phenomenon into a security problem of global proportions.

12

The Role of Women in Terrorism

With a few notable exceptions, women have played a relatively minor rôle in terrorist violence in the last few decades although conditions now are favourable for their greater involvement as free-lance non-movement-oriented terrorists as well as members of terrorist organizations. The first type refers to the individuals who commit terrorist acts, yet are not members of terrorist groups.

There is no universally accepted definition of terrorist, violence, as opposed to certain types of collective and criminal violence that at times are labelled non-political or quasi-terrorist. For the sake of uniformity in approach and clarity, let us accept the definitions of political (true) terrorism, non-political terrorism, and quasi-terrorism offered in the report on terrorism by the National Advisory Committee on Criminal Justice Standards and Goals.

Information on women as terrorist is sketchy at best. Walter Laqueur takes cognizance of the fact that women have participated in almost all guerrilla movements but have been most prominent in small urban guerrilla groups in the United States and West Germany, and particularly in Korea, where they constituted more than a quarter of the Communist revolutionary cadre.

Various mass-media sources as well as social-control sources, primarily the Federal Bureau of Investigation (FBI) and the International Association of Chiefs of Police (IACP), also concluded that women have played a relatively secondary role in terrorist violence, as well as in terrorist groups, although there have been some notable exceptions. These exceptions are discussed by Russell and Miller, who note that women have occupied an important position in West German terrorist movements, especially in the Baader-Meinhof organization and the Movement Two June where they have constituted one–third of the operational personnel.

Women as Terrorist Leaders

Women as terrorist leaders or as members of terrorist groups can be marked as follows:

Leila Khalid and Fusako Shigenobu, leaders in the Popular Front for the Liberation of Palestine (PFLP) and the Japanese Red Army (JRA), respectively. Together they were instrumental in arranging the initial PFLP training of JRA and West German cadres in Lebanon during the early 1970s.

Ellen Mary Margaret McKearney, a runner for the Irish Republican Army (IRA) bombers operating in England.

Norma Ester Arostito, cofounder of the Argentine Montoneros. She also served as their chief ideologue until her death in 1976.

Genoveve Forest Tarat, who played a key role in the 12 December 1973 Basque Fatherland and Liberty Movement (ETA-V) operation that resulted in the assassination of Spanish Premier Admiral Carrero Blanco. She also participated in the 13 September 1974 bombing of a Madried restaurant, the Cafe Rolando, which resulted in eleven dead and sevently wounded.

Margherita Cagol, the now-deceased wife of Italian Red Brigades leader Renato Curcio, who played an important role in the organization and quite possibly led the Red Brigades commando team that freed Curcio from Rome's Casale Monferrato jail on 8 February 1975.

Bernardine (Bernadette) Rae Dohm, active in the Weather Underground (WU).

Mario Torres, wife of Carlos Torres, of the Armed Forces of National Liberation (FALN). They were possibly co-leaders and co-founders of this Puerto Rican movement.

The Symbionese Liberation Army (SLA) women, including Angela Atwood, Camilla Christine Hall, Emily Mantague Schwartz Harris, Nancy Ling Perry, Mary Alice Landles, and Patricia Solytsik (alias Mizmoon-Zoya). The latter is believed to be the theoretician and homosexual lover of Camilla Hall. Both the FBI and the IACP contend that the SLA like the Weather Underground, was an organization in which homosexuality-bisexuality and pansexuality were common, characteristics present in both the ideology and practice within middle-class terrorist organizations with considerable white female input. The homosexual relationship between Hall and Solytsik is cited as an example of homosexual/ feminist orientation common within American white terrorist organizations. The SLA history also reveals a tie between white radical support of black prisoner organizations, a vague anarchic-socialist political economic orientation, feminism, and gay rights.

The Weather Underground, a group splintered from the Students for a Democratic Society (SDS), included Dohm, one of America's most sought-after terrorists. Of special interest is the fact that women factions within the WU became quite powerful and, in fact, moved into the leadership of that organization. The WU also openly espoused the need for the decline of the nuclear family and for homosexual love-both physical and emotional-to free women from male psychic and physical domination. The Weather Underground, like the SLA, espoused and practised a programme of extreme feminism, homosexuality-bisexuality, gay rights, and socialism.

Terrorist Violence by Women

We should note too that women have played a role in revolutionary and terrorist violence in the past. The following section provides a brief introduction to past incidents of terrorism by women.

According to Middendorff and Middendorff, terrorism and political murder are old forms of criminality, and female participation, at least in isolated instances, is not all that new. These two authors discuss the position that women have held in Russian revolutionary and terrorist violence. R. Gaucher points out that women played an important role in all Russian revolutionary organizations, and not only in the areas of propaganda, organization, liaison, information, and assistance: some took a direct part in terrorism. Included are four examples of violent revolutionary activities perpetrated by women, as cited by Gaucher and Middendorff and Middendorff: Tatiana Leontiev's assassination in Switzerland of a Frenchman whom she believed to be the Russian Minister of the Interior; Lydia Sture's attempted shooting of a policeman who tried to arrest her; Vera Zasulich's attempted assassination of Governor Trepov; and Vera Figner's laying of mines along a route to be taken by the Czar. Thus, one can note isolated instances of terrorist violence by women, if we examine the literature and the times of the great revolutionary upheavals. But these were isolated instances of primary middle-class women engaged in revolutionary or terrorist violence.

This class factor is a variable that holds in contemporary times as well, if we exclude the primarily lower-class nationalistic struggles of the Irish Catholics in Northern Ireland, the Basque revolutionaries in Northern Spain, and the various nationalistic struggles of East, South, and Central Africa, as demonstrated in FRELIMO's struggle in Mozambique; UNITA, MPLA, and other revolutionary groups in Angola; and the various revolutionary groups that comprised the Patriotic Front in Zimbabwe.

Middendorff and Middendorff's excellent review of changing patterns of female criminality also highlights many of the similarities and some of the differences which exist between past and contemporary female terrorists. Their comparison of Russian revolutionary women of the pre-World War I period and the German terrorists of today brings out three points: both groups of terrorists were ideologists and tried to change the course of history, although without success; both groups were from middle and upper-class families; and the Russian terrorist's demeanour in court was refined, courageous, and dignified, while the German terrorist in court exhibited extreme hostility, profanity, and discourtesy.

There can be little doubt that the North American and Western European terrorist organizations with female leadership or sizable numbers of female cadres proselytized female homosexuality and bisexuality as well as pansexualism and feminist ideology-factors not present in most South American, African, Asian, and Eastern European terrorist groups. We must not, however, confuse associative factors for causal models. Unfortunately, the data in respect to female involvement in terrorist and guerrilla organizations is rudimentary at best. Each of the above-cited explanations can and should be developed into hypotheses and tested by means of various social science research techniques. Several of the previously cited explanations grounded in the changing socio-economic role-set ascribed to women offer fruitful areas for social science research. This writer would also contend that terrorism by women may, in part, be tied to the same systemic structural-functional changes in society that have brought about uncertainty in female role-sets and a possible increase in female criminality in general.

Countless theories have been offered in an attempt to explain female criminality. Dorie Klein's excellent short review of these theoretical perspectives is certainly worth reading. It is that author's view that the same factors that have challenged and destabilized the expected traditional role-set assigned to women also have fostered terrorist activity by women.

Before going further, a brief summary of the most popular past and present theories that have attempted to explain female criminality is in order. Most of the early attempts at theory building, tried to explain female criminality in terms of physiological or psychological characteristics of individuals, with little or no emphasis on socio-cultural factors; these attempts included the theoretical work of Freud, Cesare Lombroso, and Kingsley Davis. On the other hand, W.I. Thomas and Otto Pollak created a bridge between these two broad perspectives, Chart 2 provides a summation of major theoretical perspectives of female criminality. It reveals a number of interesting perspectives shared by various social-control agencies in regard to women as terrorists; the belief that they exhibit masculine body type and psychological profiles; and the belief that many, if not most, of their acts are emotive rather than instrumental, *i.e.*, emotional rather than well-thought-out acts with a rational programme of action not tied to a love interest, such as an attempt to free a captured husband or lover from police or army custody. Social-control personnel often state that female terrorists are more likely to engage in acts of senseless or non goal-oriented violence than are their male counterparts, a factor that likely would place a disproportionate number of female terrorists into Frederick Hacker's category of crazies.

Perspectives of Female Criminality

The theoretical perspectives of female criminality can be explained as follows:

Theorist	Orientation	Title of Major Work
Cesare Lombroso	Crime as an atavism (survival of primitive traits in individuals, *e.g.*, considerable body hair) Lower intelligence Lack of passion	*The Female Offender* (New York, 1903)
W.I. Thomas	Psychological passivity Physiological immobility Women are cold and calculating Female morality Women driven by basic wishes to manipulate the male sex Drive to achieve ulterior motives Individual accommodation to social surroundings	*The Unadjusted Girl* (New York, 1923)
Sigmund Freud	Psychological passivity Physiological immobility Penis envy Women are anatomically inferior The deviant is attempt to be a man	"Anatomy is Destiny," Lectures on Psychoanalysis (New York, 1933)
E. Kingsley Davis	Demands for sexual novelty are not fulfilled in marriage Some males are cut off from sexual partners because they are unmarried, ugly, and/or deformed Some males are cut off from sexual partners because of some other sexually competitive disadvantage	"The Sociology of Prostitutes," *American Sociological Review* 2 (October 1937): 744–55
Otto Pollak	Hidden Female crime Rising crime rate among females is the result of sexual emancipation Women are as criminal as men When their criminality is detected, they may still avoid arrest Female crime is tied to socialization Some biological factors are tied to female criminality, *e.g.*, lesser physical strength than men	*The Criminality of Women* (Philadelphia, 1950)

Contd...

Theorist	*Orientation*	*Title of Major Work*
•	Psychological concomitants menstruation, pregnancy, and menopause are tied to the etiology of female crime	
M. Rappaport	Female offenders are psychological misfits	'The Psychology of the Female Offender," *NPAA Journal* 3 (January 1957): 7–12.
G. Gisela Konopka	Emotional problem: loneliness and dependency	*Adolescent Girls in Conflict* (Englewood Cliffs, NJ, 1966)
J. Cowie, V. Cowie, and E. Slater	Chromosomal explanation of female delinquency Female offenders are different physiologically and Psychologically from the normal girl Delinquent girls are more masculine than the normal girl	*Delinquency in Girls* (London, 1968)
H.C. Vedder and D. Sommerville	Female delinquency seen as blocked access or mal-adjustment to the normal feminine role	*The Delinquent Girl* (Springfield, IL, 1970)
D. Hoffman-Bustamente	Women's crime are the result of five major factors: 1. differential sex role expectations 2. sex differences in sociological pattern and application of social control 3. differential opportunities to engage in crime 4. differential access to criminal subcultures and careers 5. sex differences built into crime categories	"The Nature of Female Criminality," *Issues in Criminology* 8 (Fall 1973): 117-36
F. Adler	Greater female assertiveness Spinoff of the women's liberation movement Breakdown in prevailing patterns of sexual inequality	*Sisters in Crime* (New York, 1975)
R. Simon	Breakdown in prevailing patterns of sexual inequality Greater labour force participation of females has led to increased opportunities for crime Female criminality shall not increase drastically (Adler disagrees)	*Women and Crime* (Lexington, MA, 1975)

The following is a rudimentary attempt at a formulation of a theory of women as terrorists. It must be stressed that this theory is rudimentary at best, but it does present the known variables associated with female terrorist behaviour.

Women, except for a few notable exceptions, have played a relatively minor role in terrorist violence in the last thirty years. Official arrest and suspect data reveal a relatively minor level of female participation in terrorist activity.

Although women, except for a few notable exceptions, have played a relatively minor role in terrorist violence in the last thirty years, one may expect female participation, both as free-lance non movement-oriented terrorists as well as members of terrorist organizations, in terrorist incidents to increase dramatically in the future. Changing role-sets ascribed to women will place them more directly into the mainstream of academia and corporate enterprise. These changes in the expected belief and activity patterns of women will result in direct conflict with the more traditional female role-sets: wife, mother, and passive, gentle, non-competitive beauties of moderate or low intelligence and low aspirations, With women entering the labour force as well as the academic world at an accelerating rate, the system with its limited resources and rewards will frustrate women who have attained all of the socially defined attributes usually tied to success, such as proper speech, aggressive personalities, superior technical training, and high levels of education; these highly skilled women will perceive the reality of blocked opportunity while becoming more conscious of their unique exclusion from the system of rewards, thus fostering and reinforcing demands for socio-structural change of both a socialist and feminist nature.

We must also realize that as new employment fields open up for women, they will acquire new skills, some of which may be used in terrorist acts. Combat or combat-support units in the 'New Army' train women to shoot guns and handle explosives, while new opportunities in various local, state, and federal-level control agencies also open up similar training. Women currently taught to work on farms, in forests, and in mines learn skills in the storage and discharge of explosives.

Female input in terrorist acts is tied in Part to feminist demands and practices. Feminist organizations, or organizations with socialistic principles, allow for increased opportunities to women for upward mobility. This upward mobility more likely is determined by a woman's innate or learned skills and leadership qualities than by the sex-linked, stereotyped characteristics often found in more traditional male dominated organizations. Female input in groups that champion feminist and socialistic objectives is likely to be considerable. If such demands should exceed society's capacity to deliver reform, then violence or the threat of violence is probable by radical organizations.

Contemporary female terrorists are likely to exhibit male personality or physical traits. The demand for immediate change and the ability to compete forcefully in the labour market and in the classroom are traits often viewed as masculine. Thus, those who assert markedly radical demands for structural-functional change in regard to role-sets assigned to women, or any oppressed majority or minority, may be viewed as masculine in character. Women who lack the characteristics and traits that society considers appropriate-gentleness, passivity, non-violent personalities, seductiveness, physically attractive faces and figures–may seek success in some non-feminine realm, by displaying aggression, unadorned faces and bodies, toughness, or other masculine qualities.

Masculine or feminine characteristics are often culturally defined. Female terrorists of the future can be expected to exhibit fewer of the characteristics usually defined as masculine, because clear divisions between sex-linked roles no longer will exist.

Terrorist acts by females now and in the future will become more instrumental and less expressive. There can be little doubt that terrorist acts by females have often been expressive in character. However, as more women join terrorist groups with well-defined political goals and objectives, women will carry out fewer incidents of so-called expressive violence, or violence that does not appear to be conducive to goal achievement. There is no reason to believe that trained female terrorists will function in a manner different from trained male terrorists.

The claim that terrorism by women is often tied to the liberation of their imprisoned mates is no different from much of the terrorism perpetrated by their male counterparts. In fact, most facts of terrorism by either female or male terrorists have not been tied to the liberation of loved ones. However, male terrorism has not been totally immune to the act of struggling for the liberation of imprisoned lovers: one must recall that the Uruguayan Government's most effective counter terrorism strategy against the Tupamaros, or Movimento de Liberacion Nacional (MLN), was the wholesale arrest of the loved ones, wives, and families of the male-dominated guerrillas of the MLN movement. The government then waited for the Tupamaros to attack the jails and prisons which held their families, on the theory that during the attack the guerrillas would be slaughtered.

The emancipation of women too the household and related domestic functions, their increased opportunity and expectations in the worlds of enterprise and academia brought about by the reorganization of the workplace, and feminist pressures on women's role in the nuclear family will no doubt produce a woman who is both willing and able to take her rightful place in all aspects of society and culture, including revolutionary and terrorist activities.

Index

Q